GALL

PHOENIX ILLUSTRATED

COLIN McDOWELL

IANO

Irving Penn

For KATELL LE BOURHIS

First published in 1997 by George Weidenfeld & Nicolson Ltd

This paperback edition first published in 1998 by
Phoenix Illustrated
Orion Publishing Group,
Orion House,
5, Upper St. Martin's Lane
London WC2H 9EA

British Library Cataloguing-in-Publication Data
A catalogue record for this book is available from the British Library

ISBN 0753804972

Art Director: David Rowley
Design & typesetting: Nigel Soper
Picture Research: Joanne King

PREFACE

THIS BOOK is not a biography. It barely touches the facts of John Galliano's private life. Nor is it a full critical assessment of his work. It is still too early for that. What it sets out to provide for the reader is an examination of work in progress at a crucial point in a career. When I first approached John Galliano with the idea of a book on which we might work together, it was January 1996, and I had just seen his first couture show for the house of Givenchy. Although John was enthusiastic from the start, Dior plans meant that the book had to be postponed – for a year. In the event, it was a fortuitous delay as now, in his second year as the design director of a prestigious and well-established fashion house, he is even better placed for a retrospective review of how he reached this point. In the future, a full biography of Galliano must be written, as befits a world figure in his field. A full *catalogue raisonné* will also be necessary. At this moment, I believe this informal – but informed – account will fulfill a need. I also hope that it will go some way towards answering some of the questions and satisfying some of the immense interest that John Galliano's progress from student to head of design at Christian Dior has generated – an interest which goes far beyond the confines of the fashion world.

I have been given generous help with this book at every stage, not only by John and his team but by the many people he suggested I talk to, and the many others they in their turn suggested in order to make this book as accurate as possible. Everyone gave enthusiastically of their time, and I gathered information from John's tutors at St Martin's school of Art, his friends and his colleagues from his London years and many in Paris. Inevitably, most of the help came from John himself, not least in the matter of finding and selecting the pictures.

All the images contained in this book have been graciously contributed by the photographers themselves, and I am grateful for their cooperation. As the copyright holders, they have given authority for the images to be published on the assumption that their reproduction does not interfere with the rights of third persons to the best of their knowledge. Thanks are extended to all those who participated in the creation of these images. We have made every effort to credit all involved, but we appeal to the understanding of any we may have inadvertently overlooked.

Special thanks are due to: Amanda Harlech; Sybille de St Phalle and the staff at Givenchy; Katell le Bourhis and the staff at Dior; and Mesh Chhibber, press officer of John Galliano. David Rowley and Nigel Soper created the book's elegant design; Sarah Halliwell typed my manuscript with speed and efficiency. I thank them all.

Colin McDowell

CONTENTS

ANDREW McPHERSON

HAUNTED BY ITS APPARENT INSTABILITY, the fashion world compensates by taking itself very seriously. Conscious of the accusations of fatuity levelled at it, afraid of its own volatility, unsure of whether it is art, commerce or craft, it searches desperately for historical moments with which to anchor itself.

And it finds them: 1860, when the Englishman Worth was appointed to dress the Empress Eugénie of France and, incidentally, to found the modern world of high fashion and the cult of the mystique of the couturier; 1918, when Madeleine Vionnet showed her four-pointed dress and gave the art of dressmaking a new dimension with her experiments in cutting cloth on the bias; Mary Quant's 1955 opening of her shop, Bazaar, on the King's Road, which heralded a fashion revolution that brought the needs of the young and the casual into the fashion equation for the first time. There are others, but the fashion moment generally considered the most historic of all was specific and precise: 12 February 1947 at 10.30.

It was the moment that was, at least temporarily, to change fashion with a suddenness never previously seen, and to set it on a course that proved irresistible to women, despite initial shock, hostility and public condemnation on the highest level. On 12 February Christian Dior's 'New Look', rumoured for weeks in Paris, became a fact.

Right: An evening dress for Christian Dior haute couture, spring/summer 1997, designed by John Galliano, appears to be as delicate as a butterfly's wing, but its gossamer lightness relies on an armature which is a complex mixture of geometry and engineering. (Photo: Sarah Moon, 1997)

Previous page: photo: Lauren van der Stockt, Christian Dior archive.

The story screamed around the world. Instantly, the New Look was a scandal, an outrage, unbelievably insensitive, totally impractical. But it was also news, in a way that fashion had never been before. What had Christian Dior – mild-tempered, shy and sensitive – done to create so much fuss? Nothing more alarming than to put back the clock seven years, to where it had stopped at the beginning of the Second World War. But he had done so with a sense of style and a theatrical extravagance that made all other fashion suggestions look *démodé*. The New Look – sloping shoulders, wasp waists, padded hips and big skirts – was so convincing a statement that, within three seasons, not only were the world's couturiers following Dior's lead, but the look was also already being worn by ordinary women, to whom such extreme fashions had seemed ludicrous when they first appeared.

A moment like that will never be seen again. Fashion has moved from the autocratic base upon which it rested in those days, when French couture dictated how all fashionable women would dress. Now there is no consensus: Paris must fight for supremacy against Milan, New York and even London; and within all fashion capitals designers project widely different ideas of how women should dress, from the pared-down efficiency of minimalism and sportswear seen in New York and the eccentric eclecticism of London's fashion, to the richly wearable clothes of the Italian designers

In 1947, the 'Bar' suit was considered perfectly to encapsulate the spirit of the New Look. In 1997, John Galliano retains the New Look's confidence and glamour while adding sex, the modern fashion ingredient. (Drawing, left: Rene Gruau; right, Christian Dior spring / summer 1997 designed by John Galliano. Photo: Christian Dior archive)

and the darkly complex creations of the Japanese. Even when a certain place or time seems to encapsulate the mood of the moment, there are always maverick designers who fit into no accepted scheme: Isaac Mizrahi and Geoffrey Beene in New York; Christian Lacroix and Rei Kawakubo in Paris; Giorgio Armani and Moschino in Milan; Jasper Conran and Vivienne Westwood in London. There are few points of contact in today's fashion and, therefore, no possibility of a dominant force emanating from one designer alone, as with the New Look.

That does not mean the end of historic moments per se. They will continue to happen as long as young talent is permitted to bid for its place in the sun. One such moment occurred in January 1997, when John Galliano created his first collection as chief designer of the house of Dior.

It was an emotional occasion and, many would claim, a significant one. It marked not only the fiftieth anniversary of the New Look, but also the creative coming-of-age of John Galliano, a designer who had never failed to be controversial, and who had become a world-class figure in the years since he had graduated from St Martin's School of Art, London, in 1984.

Galliano's appointment to the most august fashion house in Paris had taken some commentators by surprise. Amidst all the rumours that sprang up on the announcement that the Italian designer Gianfranco

Creating couture clothes is a painstaking and time-consuming process which has hardly changed since Dior's day, but the efforts are all worth it in the final joy of a job well done. (Photo, left: Lauren van der Stockt; above, photo: Bellini, both courtesy, Christian Dior archive)

Ferré, who had designed the Dior collection since 1990, would not be continuing, few had seriously considered Galliano. It had seemed unlikely that he would be offered the job at Dior because only a year had elapsed since he had taken up his appointment as designer at Givenchy. Like Dior, Givenchy is part of the huge luxury conglomerate, Louis Vuitton Moët Hennessy, formed in 1987 by Bernard Arnault – the man who had placed Galliano at Givenchy and would now make the appointment at Dior.

In fact, Arnault had been negotiating Galliano's move to Dior for much of the time that Galliano had been at Givenchy. 'It was a great strain,' the designer says now. 'I couldn't tell anybody, not even my closest collaborators. I was sworn to absolute secrecy and had to go on as if nothing was happening. It was a lonely, stressful time but, in the end, it was worth it.'

Indeed it was. After years of financial uncertainty, John Galliano had been handed Paris fashion's golden apple. All he had to do was succeed. But it was not entirely clear what kind of success Bernard Arnault was looking for. The house of Dior might well be the most famous fashion establishment in the world (although most would feel that it must share that honour with Chanel – another house trading on a past based on one of the great fashion personalities, but kept vibrant by

Christian Dior took much of his New Look inspiration from the days when his mother was young. Galliano also takes the hour-glass figure – surely the most alluring female silhouette since the Minoans – and reinvents the Edwardian look in totally contemporary terms for Cleo, a bustier sheath dress of lilac taffeta overlaid with lace, a jet choker and a Masai corset. (Left: Harlingue-Viollet; right, photo: Michel Nafziger, courtesy L'Officiel, *Paris, March 1997)*

Karl Lagerfeld's bold, iconoclastic approach to modern fashion – or even the house of Saint Laurent, whose eponymous designer still managed to please and impress a large section of the fashion world). However, it had not commanded Paris since it had sacked Yves Saint Laurent, Dior's personal choice as his successor, in 1960. Arnault knew that, if the huge publicity potential of the fiftieth anniversary of the New Look were not to be thrown away, he had to choose someone who could put the spirit back into the house of Dior.

Paris felt that he would choose Jean-Paul Gaultier, a maverick guaranteed to command considerable journalistic interest. London favoured Vivienne Westwood, the notorious self-publicist who had frequently expressed her admiration of Christian Dior as a creator and a craftsman. Yet Arnault saw a potential for originality and growth in John Galliano that was not apparent in the other two – nor, indeed, in any other names mentioned in the succession hiatus.

History repeats itself in fashion as in any other field. Before being offered his own house by the textile billionaire Marcel Boussac, Christian Dior had been given the opportunity to revive the moribund Paris fashion house, Maison Philippe et Gaston, founded in 1925, which in pre-war Paris was still reasonably successful. Bought by Boussac in 1946, it had not fared well during the war, and, when Dior went to look at it in 1946, it was sadly reduced in name (and became known only as Gaston) and output (concentrating almost exclusively on furs). Above all, as Dior immediately realized, the firm's aura was hopelessly old-fashioned. In his own words, he recognized 'the impossibility of adding new wine to old bottles in a trade where true originality is all-important... I decided that I was not meant by nature to revive the dead.'

Not that there was any question for Galliano of reviving the house of Christian Dior from the dead. After Saint Laurent's exit, it had enjoyed years of quiet prosperity with Marc Bohan as its design director. Under his guidance, it had managed to retain more couture customers than any other Paris house. Under his successor, Gianfranco Ferré, it had maintained not only respectable sales, but also a respectable profile. In a sense, this was what worried Arnault. He did not want anything respectable for the anniversary of the house of Dior. He was looking for outrage, excitement, publicity and profile on the level enjoyed by Dior in 1947.

It was more complicated even than that. Whereas other contenders for the job would certainly garner publicity, it would be of the wrong sort. Westwood and Gaultier would scandalize and, inevitably, alienate. Others might be tempted to recreate the actuality of the New Look and miss the modernity he clearly wished the house to project. To work with originality in tune with the spirit of another creator while keeping

The lure of pre-revolutionary China has a powerful effect on John Galliano. There is a stillness and a fluidity in his dresses recreated under the influence of heroines like Anna Marie Wong, Gertrude Lawrence and, inevitably, Dietrich in Shanghai Express. *(Photos: Jean-Marie Perier,* Elle, *Paris, February 1997)*

your own handwriting clear is to walk on a creative knife's edge. Only the most sensitive, tactful and self-assured can have any hope of success. It was because he felt that John Galliano had this rare combination that Arnault offered him Dior.

Recreating history is not easy, nor is it required. Galliano's task was to make his own historic statement and, in order to do that, he sought out the essence of the Dior style. On 21 October 1996, at 10 o'clock, Galliano had his first appointment with Soizic Pfaff at 18 bis, rue Jean Goujon, just around the corner from the Dior headquarters in rue François 1er. Soizic was nervous. Although she had worked for Dior for some years, she had only been appointed archivist three weeks earlier. Would she be able to help the designer in the way she felt an archivist should?

The archive at rue Jean Goujon forms a fascinating adjunct to the vast Christian Dior machine at François 1er. It consists of one rather dark and hopelessly over-crowded room, the antithesis of glamour and hardly the setting for efficiency. But it contains everything anyone looking for the spirit of Dior could require. A long, deep room, one of its walls is entirely taken up by a built-in cupboard that contains the dresses from Christian Dior's time – or, at least, a good selection of them. Some are originals that have always been in the house, others are copies of key garments from his *œuvre*; many have been donated by their original clients, others bought at sales and from dealers around the world.

The remaining walls contain shelves full of books of original sketches and photographs of the creations designed for Dior's twenty-two collections. With few gaps, every dress and *tailleur* is recorded. In many cases, the record consists of a photograph taken in the atelier, showing the front and back of the garment.

For his first Dior collection, Galliano took the original spirit of the house with wit and tact by bringing his own vision to Christian Dior's 'trademark' details. (Below left, photo: Mike de Dulmen, 1957, Christian Dior archives; below right: 1954, Christian Dior archives)

Below left, Christian Dior archives; below right, Christian Dior prêt-à-porter, autumn/winter 1997–8, designed by John Galliano, photo: Christian Dior archives.

These are not glamorous fashion photographs, but 'bread-and-butter' images to record the appearance rather than the spirit of the item. Most garments are also represented by a drawing. Simple, linear and concentrating on shape rather than detail, these were produced in the atelier on press handouts.

In Dior's time, the dissemination of high fashion was far different from today. There were no designer labels, as such, and the nearest a couturier got to ready-to-wear was the range of sports and beach wear which he sold in his boutique – if, indeed, he bothered to have one. The items had nothing in common with his couture collection and were never designed by the

Dior enjoyed creating monumental shapes. Galliano translates the spirit of a sculpted evening gown by taking the inspiration of its deep, almost architectural folds to make his own statement.

maestro himself. He concentrated entirely on his couture collections, shown in January and July.

Primarily for private customers and the representatives of the world's most exclusive stores and private labels, the couture shows were shrouded in secrecy – necessarily so. There was an embargo on photographs of the clothes appearing in the press for at least six weeks after the show so that orders from customers could be executed before the impact of their novelty was dulled by press coverage. This was important for private clients, but even more important for such stores as Saks Fifth Avenue or Harrods, who bought the right to sell line-for-line copies of the original models, either under their own label, or that of the designer – in which case materials and trimmings had to be identical with those on the original model shown at the collection.

The fear was piracy. If a pirate firm – which had not proved its *bona fides*, had not been present at the collection and had not paid the considerable premium required for the right to reproduce the designs – managed to get its copies out first, it could clearly ruin the market of those who had taken the correct – and expensive – route. Because no photographer was allowed near a couture show in those days – Dior himself personally ejected a client who was discovered with a miniature camera hidden in her hat – drawings for the press, giving the minimum of detail, were an essential part of a couture house's service. It is these drawings which are held at 18 bis.

And it was these, along with the photographs, that initially excited John Galliano and his assistant, Steven Robinson. They had come to do their homework – a crash course in discovering the spirit of Dior and, as Soizic Pfaff recalls, they wanted to see everything. The

Below left: autumn/winter 1948–9, Christian Dior archives; below, Christian Dior prêt-à-porter, autumn/winter 1997–8, designed by John Galliano. (Photo: Frédéric Garcia, Christian Dior archive)

books of photographs and drawings began to sprout hundreds of yellow stickers as the men truffle-hunted through the archive. Although primarily interested in the designs created by Dior himself, they also looked at those by Saint Laurent and many of the early ones of Bohan. Soizic made hundreds of photocopies.

Determined to get the whole picture, Galliano worked in the archive for an entire week. Not satisfied, he came in for a weekend and an extra Saturday. At night he borrowed books on Dior and videos of Ferré's shows. Soizic's initial fears had been quickly dispelled. When she told Galliano how briefly she had held the job, he said, 'That makes two of us. Don't worry, we'll learn together.' She recalls how his enthusiasm never waned, even at the end of long days in the stuffy room. 'It was fascinating,' she says. 'He was so excited. He wanted to see everything. Old newspaper cuttings, press books and all the little details.'

Two of the most precious books – because they are the only ones to survive – are the *Livres de Fabrication* from 1947 and 1948, which give the technical specification of each garment in the show. A small sketch and brief description are followed by a detailed listing of materials used, the name of the garment and the names of the people responsible for making it. For example 'Bar', the most famous of all the creations shown in the first collection, was a *tailleur* consisting of a jacket in shantung and a skirt in wool. The jacket alone required 3.75 metres of shantung and 3 metres of lining. It was cut by Pierre Cardin, who worked for Dior before he opened his own establishment. (It was traditional for jackets to be cut by men and skirts to be cut by women – in this case, Monique.)

If John Galliano found such details fascinating, he found the charts that detailed the name of the garment,

Left: Christian Dior, prêt-à-porter, autumn/winter 1997–8, designed by John Galliano: the lingerie look as catwalk motif. (Photo: Christian Dior archives)

its model, *vendeuse* and customer even more so. Above all, he found the swatches of material which were pinned to the charts deeply moving. He pored over colours and textures of fabrics left largely undisturbed for fifty years. He had discovered the essence of a Christian Dior creation – the raw material that excites, stimulates and challenges the true couturier.

And, of course, there was the joy of closely examining the made-up garment in the cupboard. The two men were not content merely to look and touch. They needed to analyse and itemize what made a Dior creation unique. Several key garments were taken to the studio in order for the designer to fully study them from every angle.

In this, Soizic had a problem. She felt she was letting them down because she had so few examples of *flou*, light dressmaking as opposed to tailoring, which created the spectacular ballgowns that were one of the strongest statements in Dior's collections during the fifties. Most of the really magnificent examples were in New York, on loan to the Metropolitan Museum of Art for the major Dior retrospective mounted to coincide with the fiftieth-anniversary celebrations. The best of the rest were required for 'Christian Dior Spirit', a spectacular one-evening-only show arranged by Katell le Bourhis and Gianfranco Ferré for the Dior Gala on 9 December in New York. As the new designer for Christian Dior, John Galliano was present at the gala and, as Soizic Pfaff says, 'He clearly worked when he was in New York. He came back wanting to see even more details.'

The search for the spirit of Dior was almost complete.

But there were two more vital pieces required to complete the picture. Of one, John Galliano was aware. The other was to be a serendipitous discovery.

Les Signes de Reconnaissance de la Maison Christian Dior is a thick, spiral-bound book for use only within the company. It isolates the components that make up the style of the house of Dior, dealing with the fabric and furnishing of the house: the colours, textures and inspirations of Dior, and the accessories and publicity which add strength to the griffe, or label. It is, perhaps, an analysis that could be made by anyone who bothered to take the time to examine the house set up by Dior, but it is an invaluable and speedy form of induction for the tyro in the firm.

Starting with the famous grey-and-white colour scheme based on the Louis XVI period, chosen by Dior for its simplicity, sobriety and classicism, as well as for its cool elegance that bespoke Paris for him, *Les Signes de Reconnaissance* examines the components of the décor of Avenue Montaigne. Created for Dior by Victor Grandpère, these include: the famous little gilt salon chairs with their wicker seats, the grey-and-white armchairs, the pearl-rimmed oval medallion

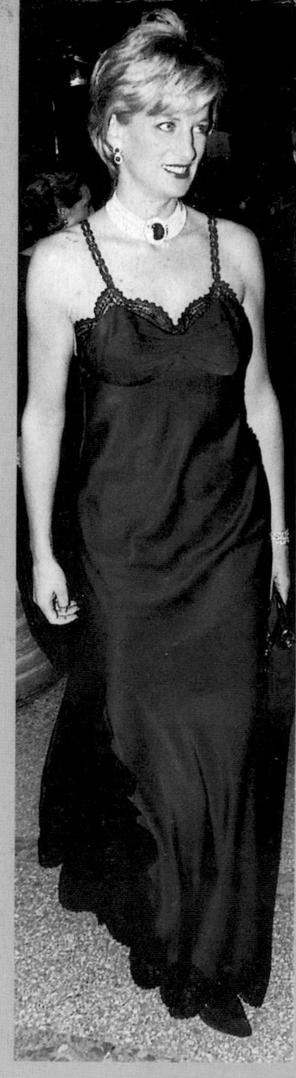

The first Galliano dress for Dior was a lingerie-look creation for the Princess of Wales (right), who was guest of honour at the Metropolitan Museum of Art, New York, in December 1996. Left: John Galliano's original sketch for the dress. (Photo, right: Rex Features)

containing the firm's logo. The book looks at Dior's favourite flowers – the rose and, pre-eminently, the lily of the valley, used as the basis for his perfume, Diorissimo, which was created by Edmond Roudniska in 1956 – and his colours: soft pinks, pearl greys – which Dior felt were 'très Paris' – reds, and 'glorious black', which he considered the supreme colour of elegance.

Dior divided fabrics into the masculine and feminine. The former, predictably enough, were largely what he called the 'English' fabrics: hound's-tooth check, Prince of Wales check and all the fabrics worn by the Duke of Windsor. (In Dior's day, the Duke was considered the archetypal British dandy, renowned for the Savile Row perfection of his appearance, even though his clothes were by no means all from the home of traditional sartorial elegance.) Above all, Dior loved pinstripes, the uniform of the English establishment, because for him, they symbolized '*l'élégance brittanique*', which had always so impressed him.

The feminine fabrics were as French as the masculine were British. Crepe, tulle, organza and lace

A couturier's creativity is open to all stimuli and the decorative appeal of ethnic dress is considerable. However, it takes a strong imagination and a sure hand to avoid a result that might look patronizing. Galliano, here, adapts ethnic details to haute couture, avoiding all the pitfalls and retaining the powerful images of photographer Mirella Ricciardi, which are a continuing influence on John Galliano. (Left, photo: Peter Lindbergh; above: Mirella Ricciardi)

– both *dentelle* and *guipure* – were the basis of the soft fluidity of Dior's romantic day dresses and the medium of some of the most magnificent evening dresses created this century. In Dior's hands, they were used to unite femininity and grandeur in a memorably theatrical way. Even today, photographs of Dior's grand ballgowns of the fifties move us by their authority as much as their beauty. It isn't hard to imagine Galliano's excitement as he pored over the pages of *Les Signes de Reconnaissance*, especially when he knew that several superb examples hung in Soizic's long cupboards waiting to be examined with painstaking attention to detail.

The Orient excited Parisian aristic and social circles from the late nineteenth century up to the 1920s. A hundred years later John Galliano follows in the footsteps of Degas and Manet in his recreation of a cultural mood for Christian Dior's Prèt-a-Porter autumn/winter 1997–8 advertising campaign, on which he worked as creative director, with photographer Nick Knight, art director Peter Saville, and model Shalom Harlow. (Photo: Nick Knight)

Exciting as his discoveries were, none was especially surprising. But, in his researches into the final famous element in the Dior vocabulary, the leopard print first shown in 'Jungle', a day dress, and 'Africaine', a leopard-printed evening dress, on 12 February 1947 – and a feature of the Dior look from that moment – he discovered what was perhaps the most important element for him. His eye was arrested by a photograph taken by Cecil Beaton of a woman of supreme elegance, a woman of a certain age, a woman of total style. Wearing a leopard-skin coat, pushed slightly away from her shoulders to reveal a five-strand rope of pearls, with a leopard-skin turban with a veil, and sparkling diamonds at her wrist, she seemed the personification of the elegance of the house of Christian Dior for which John Galliano had been subconsciously searching.

The new young designer had discovered the legendary Mitzah Bricard. A woman of extravagant taste and extraordinary chic, totally cosmopolitan, a woman of the world, Germaine Bricard, always known as Mitzah, was, in Dior's own words, 'one of those increasingly rare people who make elegance their sole *raison d'être*'. She had worked in the thirties as a social and fashion adviser to Edward Molyneux, the British couturier in Paris renowned for his elegantly understated tailoring which, Dior admitted, had enormously influenced him. Originally appointed by Dior to oversee the millinery department – an area of extreme importance in the days when no *tailleur* was deemed complete without a chic hat – the influence of her taste went beyond hats, and informed the whole establishment. As Dior said, 'I knew that her presence in my house would inspire me towards creation.'

Leopard prints were a Dior trademark from his first show. Galliano gives them a completely new feeling by combining leopard with lace to produce a potent evening look: half-bedroom, half-jungle in its appeal. Nicole Kidman photographed by Karl Lagerfeld for Vanity Fair *wearing a Christian Dior haute couture dress from the spring/summer 1997 collection designed by John Galliano. (Photos: above, Nepo, 1947, Christian Dior archive; right: Karl Lagerfeld)*

A design idea can be recreated in many moods. 'Eloise' (right), created by Christian Dior in 1948, was revised by Marc Bohan in 1980 as the source for a spectacular orange cape, and both were combined by Galliano in 1997 to produce 'Kamata', a totally original reworking of the theme. Left, Christian Dior haute couture, spring/summer 1997, designed by John Galliano (Photos: left, Michael Thompson, Vogue, *Paris, March 1997 right: Christian Dior archive)*

Mitzah Bricard's great contribution to Dior, apart from her impeccable taste, was the fact that she knew precisely how a woman should dress in order to please a man – which, in the forties and fifties, was the point and privilege of women who dressed at couture level. She had been one of the great courtesans of Paris in the interwar years, a successor to the *grandes horizontales* of the Belle Epoque and therefore a link with that period of 'figures muffled in furs, gestures *à la* Boldini, bird of paradise plumes and amber necklaces'. This was the period that had so enraptured Dior, together with the memories it stirred of his mother. It also entranced John Galliano and Steven Robinson in their search for a romantic ideal.

They fell in love with the idea of Mitzah Bricard as a distant but powerful muse, their imaginations fired by the tales of her stylish attitudes: how she had been the mistress of a Russian prince, who showed his infatuation by showering her with pearls; how she wore a scarf tied at her wrist to disguise the scar left after a suicide attempt in the early days when she was young and vulnerable. Above all, they were attracted by her superb *ex cathedra* comments, such as her dismissal of society women whom, she felt, had brought down the profession of the *demi-mondaine* because, 'They'll go to bed for a *café crème*'. This was all from a woman who spent her days either at Dior or in the Ritz and loathed the countryside – when asked who was her favourite florist, she unblinkingly replied, 'Cartier'.

Through her, Galliano and Robinson moved back to Dior's mother and the tightly waisted, elegantly shaped silhouettes of their favourite period: those marvellous years of the new century before the First World War when high life, for the grotesquely over-privileged and pampered, produced fashionable attitudes that lasted long after the money and power that had originally sustained them had been swept away. It was the world of flash and dazzle; the world in which great jewellers such as Cartier thrived; the world when the grand hotels were at their grandest; the world where no discomfort was too great, provided the end result was *le dernier cri* of fashionable luxury. It was a world already known and loved by John Galliano through the paintings of John Singer Sargent and Boldini.

It was that world which connected him to the spirit of Christian Dior. At the end of his research with the archivist Soizic Pfaff, John Galliano was ready to create the collection which, while being as modern as he could make it, would be a romantic homage to the memory of Dior himself, and all of Dior's own memories in turn, which had given the famous New Look collection such an impact in 1947.

But that wasn't all that 18 bis, rue Jean Goujon had revealed. While researching there daily John Galliano had begun to realize that he and Dior had much more in common than the new designer could have imagined when he had signed his contract with Bernard Arnault. Dior had been young in the twenties, when Paris was at the cutting edge of artistic excitement, a time of creative and sexual licence when young men could live their lives on a carefree level of hedonism with no one

Lace was a Dior signature which he used with clotted-cream richness to create lady-like effects. Galliano updates the mood with his sexy white, lace-leather short sundress for summer 1997. Left, 1957; right, Christian Dior haute couture, spring/summer 1997, designed by John Galliano. (Photos: left: Christian Dior archives; right: Michael Thompson)

added the unexpected ethnic touch of Masai jewellery, which lifted the collection away from nostalgia and made it the most strongly directional statement of the fashion season.

And the direction was exactly parallel to that of Dior's first collection, fifty years previously: towards seduction. Galliano's concept of femininity was about woman as *femme fatale*, as huntress and heroine, proud of her sexuality and at ease with her power. Constantly, with tact and grace, references were made to the original vision of Dior as seen by the modern eyes of Galliano: 'Diorbella', a hound's-tooth suit in black and white with a 'Mitzah' lilac lining; 'Diorla', a sleeveless crepe dress in ivory. The first seventeen outfits, for '*Jour, Déjeuners et Voyages*', all had names that played on 'Dior' – including some awkward ones such as 'Gallidior' – to emphasize the link.

But it was the '*Fin d'après-midi*' and '*Soir, grands soirs et bals*' sections which showed that Galliano was master – of himself, of Dior and of Paris. The audience became increasingly excited as the models appeared: 'Kitu', a mermaid dress in flower-painted silk taffeta; 'Kimoja', a jungle-green bias-cut sheath under a spectacular multi-coloured parrot feather cape; 'Cleo', an Edwardian sheath of jet-embroidered lilac taffeta with a jet Masai corset; 'Mitzah', a lilac silk, tulle and organza evening gown in the grandest fifties manner, and, most spectacular of all, 'Kamata', a brilliant orange and fire evening gown with trailing skirts and layers of petticoats worn with a Masai plate necklace and breastplate. Then, 'Paloma', the wedding dress that traditionally always ends any couture collection, in pleated white chiffon, organza feathers and bird heads, and it was all over, the long hours and many weeks of work, shown briefly and once only, in less than thirty-five minutes.

The Galliano for Dior couture show at the Grand Hotel had been spectacular. Conceived on a lavish scale, it was full of superlatives even without the clothes. Whereas other designers showed in the ballroom, the Dior show used most of the hotel's ground floor, which was turned into a facsimile of the décor of the Dior showroom in Avenue Montaigne, including its famous staircase on which luminaries such as Cocteau and Dietrich had been happy to sit in Dior's shows in the fifties. It was a lavish gesture calculated to impress the world with Bernard Arnault's confidence in his young protégé.

Clearly, money had been spent: 791 gold chairs were arranged in two rows so that all the guests were close enough to the models to feel as involved as they would have been in an original Dior show; the salons were decorated with magnificent flower arrangements using 4,200 roses; the walls were covered with 800 metres of grey Dior fabric. It had taken 146 people thirty-six hours to transform the hotel into a *maison de*

couture and, behind the scenes, 50 mannequins, 50 dressers, 16 hairdressers and 15 make-up artists had worked for over eight hours to make sure that every model looked totally perfect as she stepped out to face the crowd which, together with the gate-crashers, numbered well over a thousand.

In their number were fashion's movers and shakers, the editors of the great magazines, the fashion writers, the social commentators and the cream of Parisian social and political life, all of whom the house of Dior hoped would return to buy – as, indeed, many did. *Women's Wear Daily* reported that the day after the show, Dior's three couture salons had been filled to capacity with appointments from half-past eight in the morning to after seven o'clock at night, and Caroline Grouvel, Directrice de Couture, had been forced at times to allow fittings in her office, from which, in between, she reported that the bestsellers were the ballgowns, which were being ordered in white, to be worn as wedding gowns.

The press were equally as enthusiastic. *The New York Times* declared, 'Among Couture Debuts, Galliano's is the Stand Out', and continued, 'Mr Galliano's show was a credit to himself… to Mr Dior… and to the future of the art'. *Il Messaggero* claimed, 'Here in Paris, Fashion Speaks English.' *Women's Wear Daily* considered that, 'Galliano's Fashion Moment' had 'all the right ingredients: beauty, direction and more than enough drama to keep the fashion flock in a tizzy', and the *International Herald Tribune*, praising Galliano's 'divine madness', said, 'Surely Galliano's 16-year career has been a dress rehearsal for this sublime moment?' Most extravagant of the accolades came two months later with the all-important collections issues of the great fashion magazines: Galliano's clothes featured on the front covers of the March issues of *French Vogue*, *Elle*, *Marie Claire* and *L'Officiel*, as well as *Time* magazine.

John Galliano had come home on what the *International Herald Tribune* called his 'indelible images of magic and romance'. As he appeared to take his curtain call in scenes that the London *Daily Mail* felt were 'a bit like a coronation', many in the audience, remembering the comment of his friend André Leon Talley on his appointment to the house of Givenchy – 'I don't think John is going to start wearing grey flannel double-breasted suits' – were surprised to see him wearing a suit in Dior Prince of Wales grey and a hat to cover his newly removed dreadlocks. It was John Galliano's personal homage to the man who had founded Maison Dior so brilliantly fifty years previously.

Christian Dior, together with Mitzah Bricard, the couturier's muse and a continuing inspiration to his successor, John Galliano, who stands in front of a Dior forme on his 36th birthday. (Left, photo: Bellini, Christian Dior archive; right, photo: Bertrand Rindoff and Frédéric Garcia, Christian Dior archive)

CLOSE-UP: Creating the Collection

IS IT BECAUSE JOHN GALLIANO felt so isolated when he went to school in England after the warmth and ubiquity of the extended family life of the Mediterranean that his fashion 'family' is so important to him? Certainly, he needs his collaborators to be close and deeply involved with everything he does. Jeremy Healy, his music guru, has been a friend for more than twelve years. Amanda Harlech was Galliano's imaginative right hand from 1984 until his move to Dior in 1996. She and her husband had frequently slept on the floor of John's first workroom in the East End. When working on a collection, she had brought along her babies and popped them on a shelf to play with bolts of fabric while she got on with the process which Galliano has described as 'making all the madness sublime'. When John moved to Paris, she commuted from the fastnesses of Shropshire, where she lived a life of unimpeachable rusticity, to help him reveal 'the beauty, line, grace, humility and outrage that is burning in his clothes'.

Amanda Harlech's notebook of a collection – both an aide-mémoire *and an inspiration*

Sibylle de Saint Phalle, who began by modelling for him, remained by Galliano's side through the difficult London years and also joined him in Paris. Steven Robinson, who came to Galliano for a student placement in 1988, seems likely to remain with John for ever. He is so attuned to the designer that he is claimed by everyone, including John, to be his alter ego. Bill Gaytten, cutter and technical adviser, has been with John since the Fallen Angels collection, with only three years out in the mid-eighties. Collaborators cling to John Galliano.

The thing which cements them together is creative intensity. As Gaytten says, 'He is so imaginative. He gives you chances you wouldn't get anywhere else. You just have to look at the clothes to see that. They're not exactly Ralph Lauren. Where else would you get the chance to make a dress out of safety-pins – and not just cobbled together, but with all the passion that goes into any other dress?'

Just as every John Galliano show is a palimpsest of sources and stimuli, so every dress has a multi-layered history and speaks to fashion cognoscenti on several levels. According to Amanda Harlech, the original idea – for shows and collections – invariably comes from the designer. It can be something as inchoate as a colour, a

Couturiers are always ready to take risks in order to push fashion forward. For his own-label, autumn/winter 1997, prêt-à-porter collection Galliano proved that shapely and sophisticated garments can be created from the humblest of materials – in this case safety pins. (Photos: above, Patrice Stable Agency; left, photos in John Galliano's sketchbooks for his prêt-à-porter autumn/winter 1997–8 collection include ones by Mario Testino and Irving Penn)

John Galliano's visual research ranges over many cultures and periods. Every item that interests him is collected in sourcebooks to be used as possible future stimuli. Intensely personal, they give a unique insight into the creative process which makes a Galliano collection a sophisticated multi-level statement.

All fashion designers are eclectic 'borrowers', throwing wide their nets in the search for inspiration. Galliano marshalls his ideas for a collection in sourcebooks which contain visual references of anything that has stimulated his imagination and will help to unfold the 'story' of his clothes.

Santa Casilda by *Zurbarán, a source of inspiration for* Balenciaga.

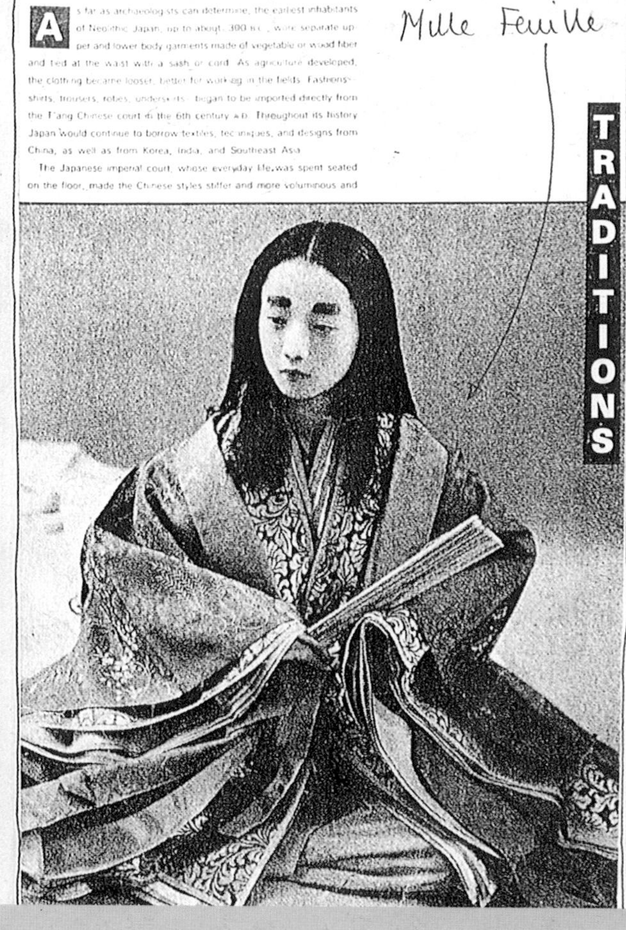

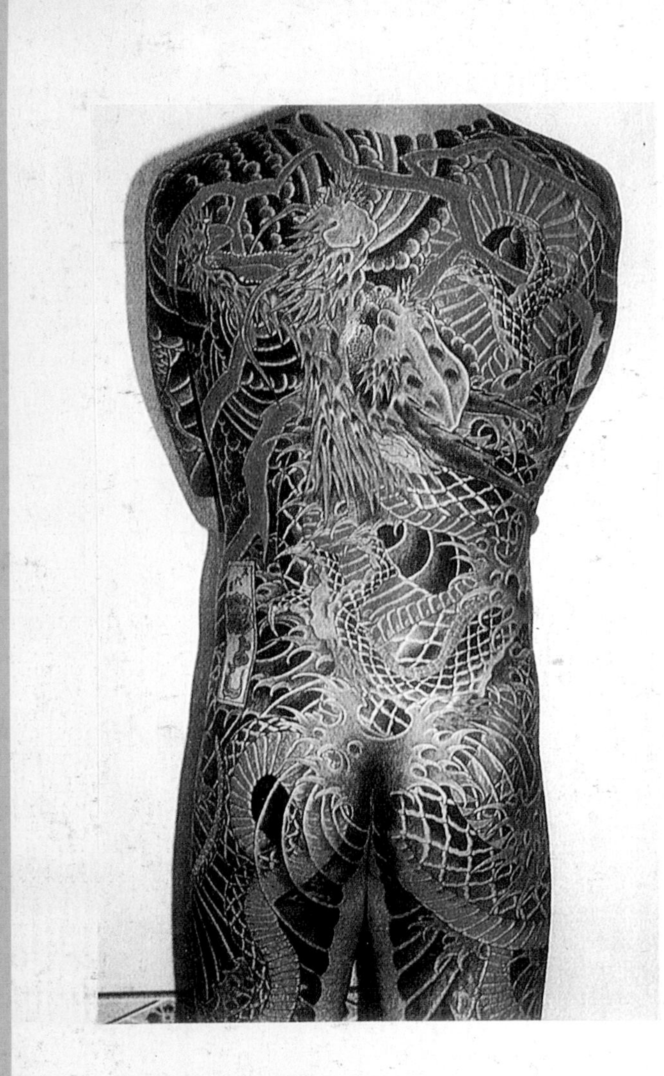

In the same autumn/winter 1997–8, prêt-à-porter show, tattoos and Egypt figure heavily as influences, which merge to create something entirely new. (Photos, right: Anthea Simms)

texture, or even one word for the imagination to latch on to. Steven Robinson says it can start to form as a story in John's head as much as a year ahead. 'It's a slow process,' he concedes. 'We don't all sit down and say, "Right, we've got to think of a story." Somehow, it all comes together naturally when we're researching.'

'John and I used to have endless conversations – often by telephone,' Amanda adds, "... What happens if she has a lilac velvet ribbon?"... "Yes, and black jet beading on the edge of the bodice"... "And she's in the forest, isn't she?"... "Yes, and... " They were marvellously exciting moments. And the story was always there, in John's head. And all the answers came out in the clothes. It's a question of ordering. It's like stringing beads. That was my job really, helping to bring the beads together into a story necklace.' She refers nostalgically to 'the explorative joys of working with John. He was always the one who discovered the right painter or historic character as a basis for the story.'

Just as it is generally known that every Galliano collection has a story, whether for his own label or for Givenchy or Dior, it is no secret that he and his team spend considerable amounts of time in background research in order to create a world in which they can begin to design clothes. Much of the research is done in London. John and Steven spend a week at the beginning of each season steeping themselves in the

culture they know the best. As Steven says, 'More and more, we need to take in London. We visit London six to eight times per year, to get its spirit. We use the streets, the clubs, the libraries.' John explains further: 'We split London up by neighbourhood and then we leave ourselves entirely open. We always go to the markets – Camden, Portobello – and the V&A. We check out the bookshops and the exhibitions. Might go to the ballet or a musical. And we rely heavily on friends who can bring us into the picture and tell us what's what. Of course, there's clubbing – that's when I hook up with my old mates. I still party, but not as much as I did. In Paris, we're all working so hard that I have to lay the law down and say to the team, "Look, we *must*

The decorative extravagance of circus costume, especially when heightened by Hollywood's glamour machine, as in the 1952 film The Greatest Show on Earth, *starring Gina Lollobrigida as a tightrope artiste, is a rich source of inspiration for exotic decorative effects, including embroidery. (Right, for John Galliano, spring/summer 1997, Nadja Auermann wears a carousel horse Lesage embroidered silk tulle evening dress, photo: Niall McInerney)*

'He has a luminious quality which makes him unique in fashion: poetry, fantasy, magic, beauty – he dares to make us dream.'

– STEPHANE MARAIS

Icons of style and beauty feed the imagination of all couturiers. Givenchy's muse, Audrey Hepburn, was equally as inspiring for Galliano when he became design director for the house of Givenchy in 1995. (Photo: Andrew McPherson)

go out on Friday night. There's only four more Fridays before the collection!" But it has to be timetabled. Everything does now. A normal day starts at eight in the morning and can easily go on until ten at night. And there might be as many as twenty appointments in a day. I do ten collections a year. But London's different. I go with Jeremy on gigs. He takes me clubbing up north a lot now. Manchester... Liverpool... I love the clubs up there. They have a raw, driving energy. Very positive and strong. At the end of the week we come back to Paris with books, videos, antiques, old clothes – and minds buzzing with anticipation.'

Once their minds are ordered, John and Steven begin to build up the research books for the collection, creating pages from all the things which have stimulated them and totting up a visual storyboard. There will be postcards; photocopies; pages from books; pieces of fabric; Polaroids taken in museums or on the streets, scribbled notes by their side. The story does not always start with a woman, and the pages of the research book mix several atmospheres, cultures and historic eras. There are recurring themes, which often cross-reference with other collections, but the process is never formulaic.

'It's a very impressionistic approach,' John says. 'It's a dialogue between past and present. The starting point is usually factual, but we allow our imaginations to run riot. The story happens differently each time. Certain things begin to go around in my head and then we start to embroider on them. For example, the last Galliano show linked punk, Egypt and Theda Bara with uniforms and anti-establishment behaviour. And we kept getting coincidences. Somebody would say, "Did you know that Siouxsie Sioux of Siouxsie and the Banshees was obsessed with Theda Bara?" Then you think, "Oh! It's *so* right!" There's a story. So that's what you give to the team and they go off and do *their* research. They come back. "It was made of turquoise." "No it wasn't. It was lapis lazuli. I've checked. I went to the Louvre." All the time, the skeleton of the story is being clothed with layers of richness.'

The narrative once begun, different people get different parts of the tale. About six weeks before the show, John will say to Steven something like, 'There is this woman, born and bred in Russia and she runs away...' and then they're off. The story is taken up. 'This section needs to look like this,' gesturing to various pages in the research books. 'No, it needs to be

Writers have notebooks, composers music paper on which to work out their thoughts. For the dress designer it is a blank sheet of paper on which he formulates his ideas, but by the time the design is finalized it has become a crucial document, telling its own complete story.

As a collection takes shape, every outfit, identified by a number, is drawn with notes for the cutters in the atelier, along with fabric samples, Polaroids, or anything else which helps to bring the drawing towards the final three-dimensional creation – even the name of the model who will wear it.

more theatrical.' 'Well, *she* has to be theatrical. She's a screen goddess!' 'Its only a *B*-movie!' 'But she's given her all!' It sounds fun, even child-like, but this is a vital part of the creative chain – as Galliano says, 'It helps us to paint a rounded picture of the heroine and inspires us to develop the different looks in the collection.'

In the next stage John will call Jeremy and tell him the story. They won't discuss music at this point. It will be, 'This is how I'm beginning to feel about the collection.' Then drawings, photocopies, swatches and

Christian Dior autumn/winter 1997, designed by John Galliano (Photos: Anthea Simms)

storyboards are sent over to London and Jeremy begins his research, working in much the way that John and Steven do, ranging as widely as possible over opera, eighteenth-century chamber music, jazz, rap and pop classics. He then mixes a test cassette to which John listens frequently and very attentively. The two men have worked closely for so many years that it is rare for John to reject anything, and soon the running order of the show is worked out in conjunction with the music. Steven believes that Jeremy's interpretation brings a vital element to the collection which sometimes makes John rethink certain things. Amanda Harlech agrees, saying that Jeremy Healey's input is vital: 'The music is like a multi-layered, rich, rich, rich carpet which mixes the savage and rarefied, as John's clothes do,' but she also adds, 'John has total faith in himself. Deep down, the core – the white heat, volcanic creativity – is all John's. Nobody can dampen that fire and, in a sense, that is what makes the rest rather unnecessary. It's *his* creative spark that matters. Of course, the team is important, but it is he who has the spark and the team hasn't.'

Inspired by the past, John Galliano makes a contemporary statement involving reworking the spirit of the original rather than slavishly copying its decorative forms. Shape and volume define a period more clearly than detail does. (Left: Givenchy haute couture, autumn/winter 1996–7, designed by John Galliano, photo: Paolo Roversi)

Nevertheless, as if to emphasize the coherence of the team, everyone involved admits that there is no such thing as a meaningful job description. 'Shared viewpoints mean more than job descriptions,' Vanessa Bellanger, Steven's assistant, insists. Of American and French parentage, she studied law and is able to bring attitudes not found in other members of the team. 'We are reference points for John,' she says. 'We're there to do whatever he needs to have done – which varies daily, even by the hour. It is a high-octane creative situation. You don't think about what your job is. You think, "What needs to be done?" Not for you. Not for your role. For John.'

He needs all the help available in order to prevent the pressure becoming too much. Even in between meetings and fittings there is almost always someone waiting for him to check something, or make a decision. In a sense, it is a self-imposed pressure, but a necessary one. As Steven Robinson points out, 'John controls everything, at every step. For instance, even though we've decided on shoe colours, John will check *every* shoe, down to the colour of the buckle. Nothing goes through until he has personally checked it – the buttons, the linings, *everything*. He goes into the atelier when everyone has gone home and personally checks. It's high-energy input from him all day.'

There is a basic structure to any collection. Even before designing begins, certain areas are pre-ordained. There must be day, cocktail, and evening wear, and that pattern underpins all creative

John Galliano's own-label dress from his autumn/ winter 1995–6 prêt-à-porter show (right), worn by Kate Moss, displays the influences from his reference books, seen above and overleaf. (Photo, right: Patrice Stable Agency)

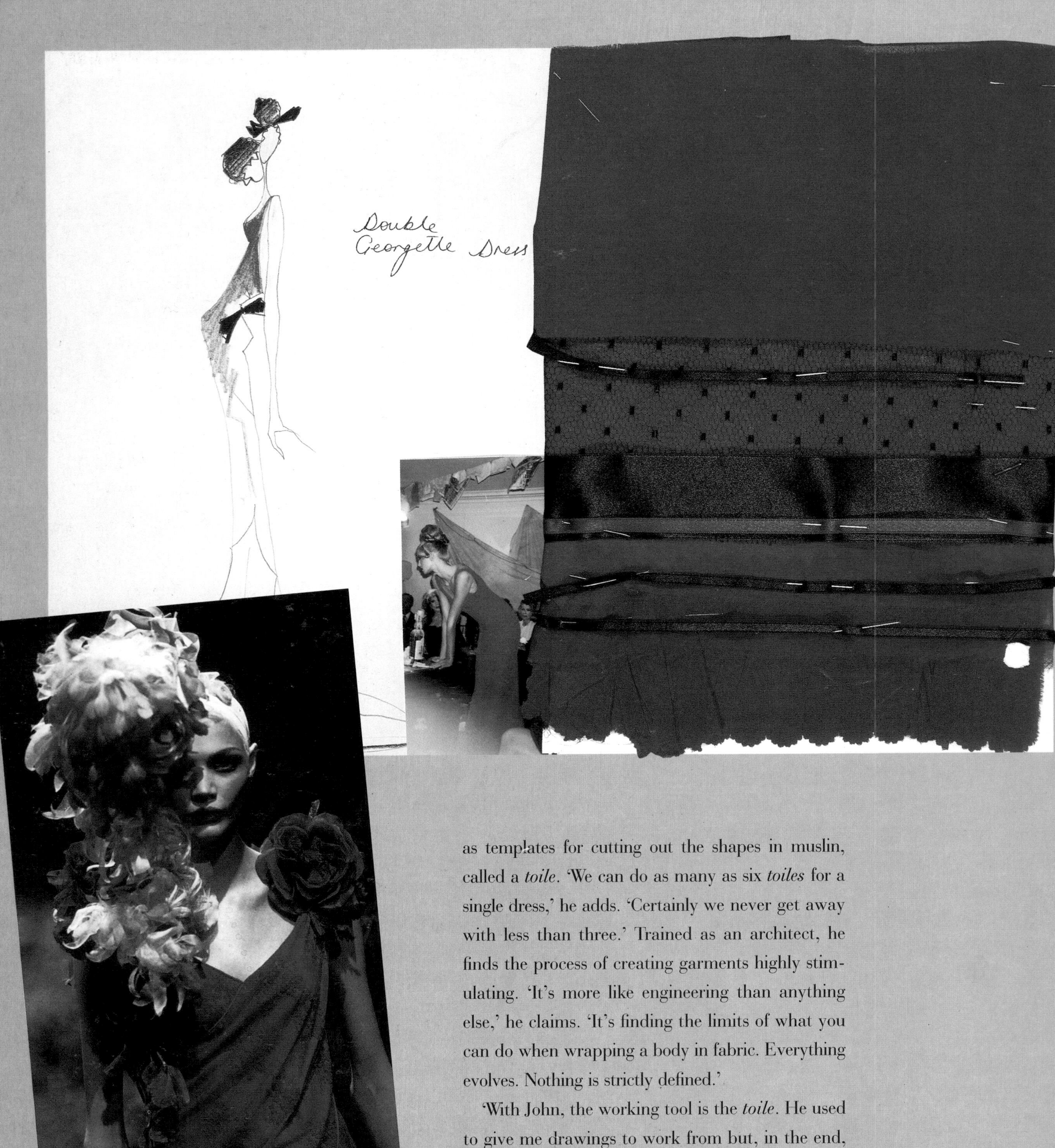

as templates for cutting out the shapes in muslin, called a *toile*. 'We can do as many as six *toiles* for a single dress,' he adds. 'Certainly we never get away with less than three.' Trained as an architect, he finds the process of creating garments highly stimulating. 'It's more like engineering than anything else,' he claims. 'It's finding the limits of what you can do when wrapping a body in fabric. Everything evolves. Nothing is strictly defined.'

'With John, the working tool is the *toile*. He used to give me drawings to work from but, in the end,

Overleaf: From John Galliano's own-label collection, autumn/ winter 1995–67. (Photo, Mario Testino)

the *toiles* would bear no relation to them, so we don't bother now. I work on the more fantastic dresses. The most interesting part is the actual cutting. I'm excited by the ideas, the passion and fantasy of it all. John is the one who keeps pushing the barriers forward. You don't have to know how to cut in order to design brilliantly. I've never seen John cut or sew *anything*. His great skill, apart from his imagination, is in encouraging and enthusing. It's always, "Why can't we? *Why* can't we do it?" He's very hard-headed and determined for a man who conceives such romantic dresses. We have to bash an idea around for a long time before we give up. It's usually only time that's allowed to beat us. And that is the ever-present enemy.' Even the most basic, bias-cut dress using between four and five metres of fabric will require two dressmakers to work on it for a week – and spending 150 hours on something complicated is no out of the way thing.

No one begrudges the time. The only regret is that there is not enough of it.

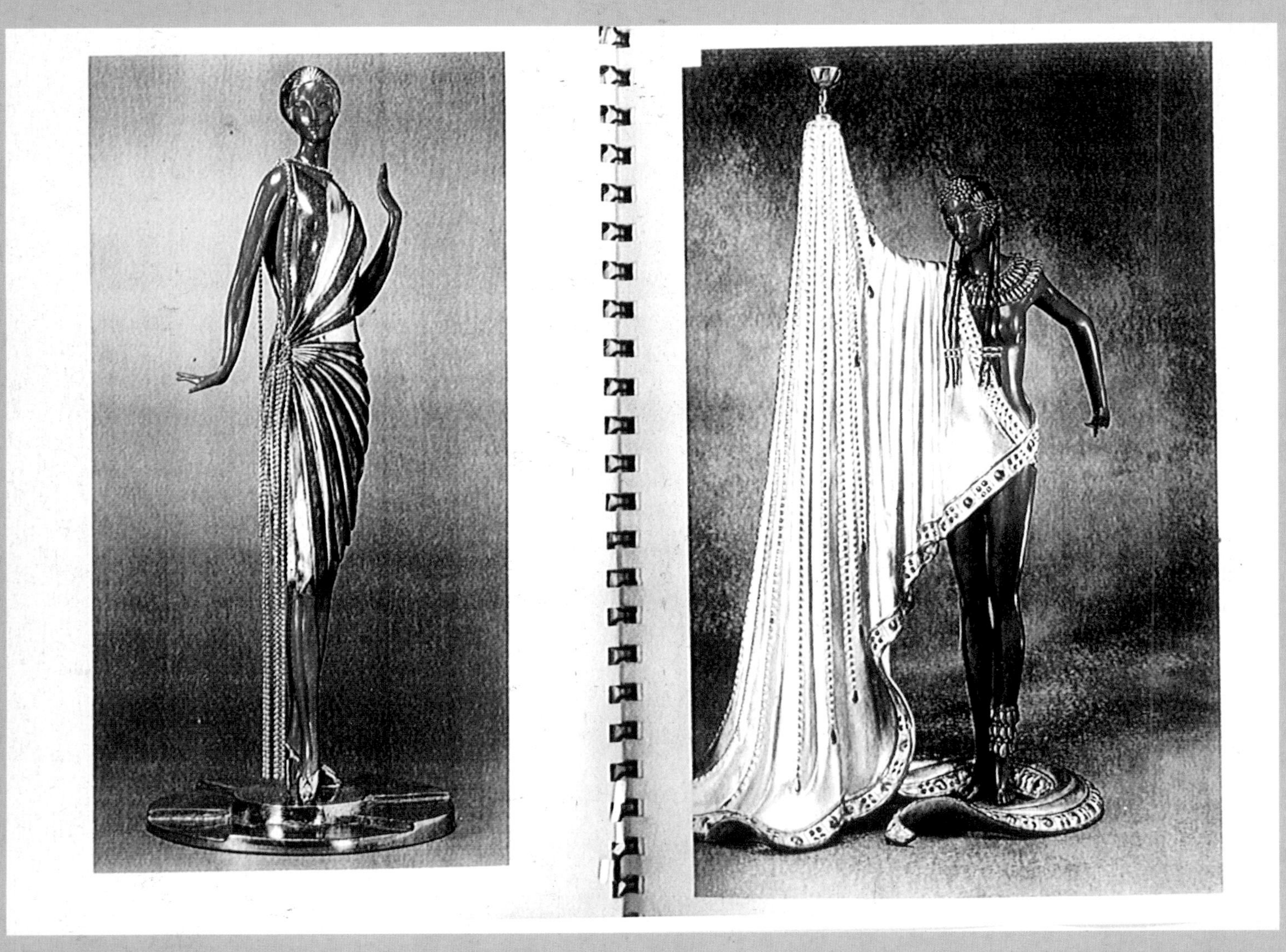

Erté's draped figures seem far removed from Galliano's bold exercise in the Nile mode as worn by actress Milla Javovich (seen here with film director Luc Besson) at the 1997 Cannes Film Festival, but the spirit, if not the material, is identical. (Photo: Bertrand Rindoff Petroff)

Behind the scenes in a couture house is a mixture of the exotic and the utilitarian as skilled hands turn a dream into practical reality. Starting with the patterns (above), and ending with the final fitting, the process involves dedication and perseverance at all stages. (Photos: Andrew McPherson)

Overleaf, photo: Lauren van der Stockt, Christian Dior archive.

WHO'S AFRAID
JOHN GALLIANO

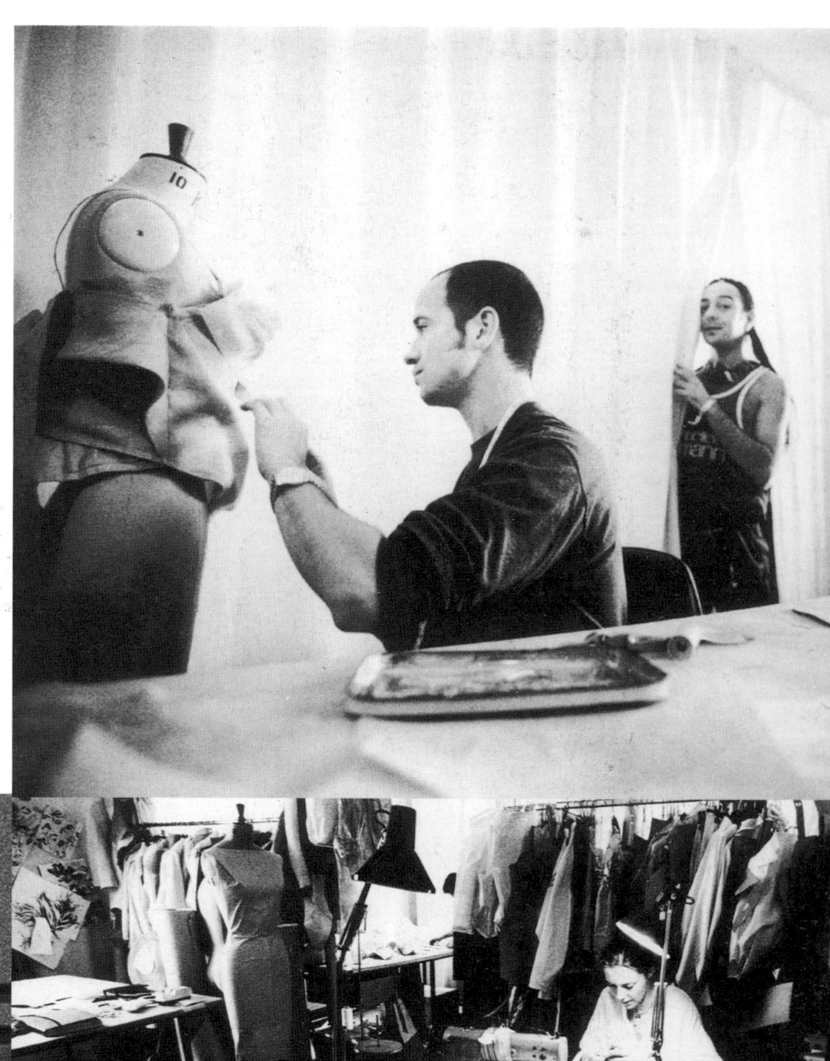

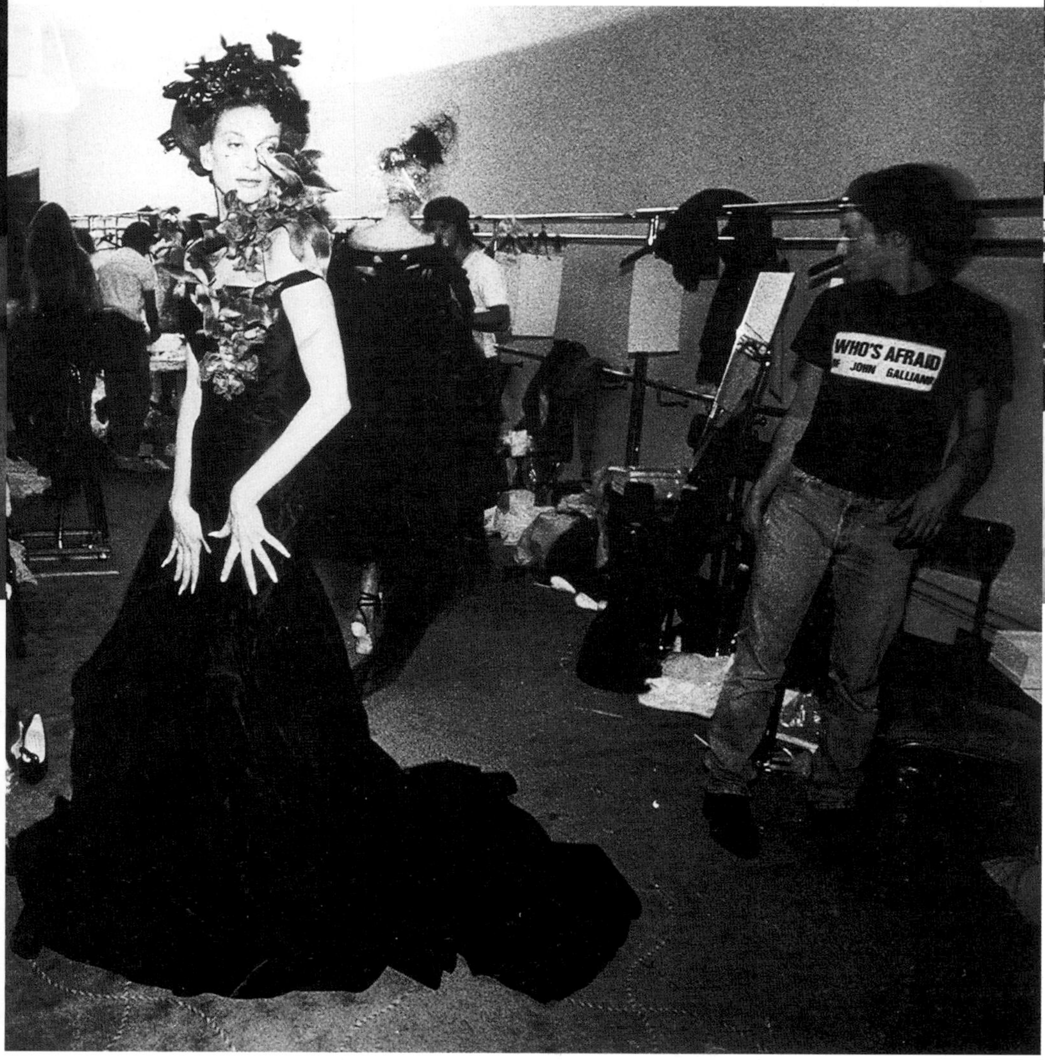

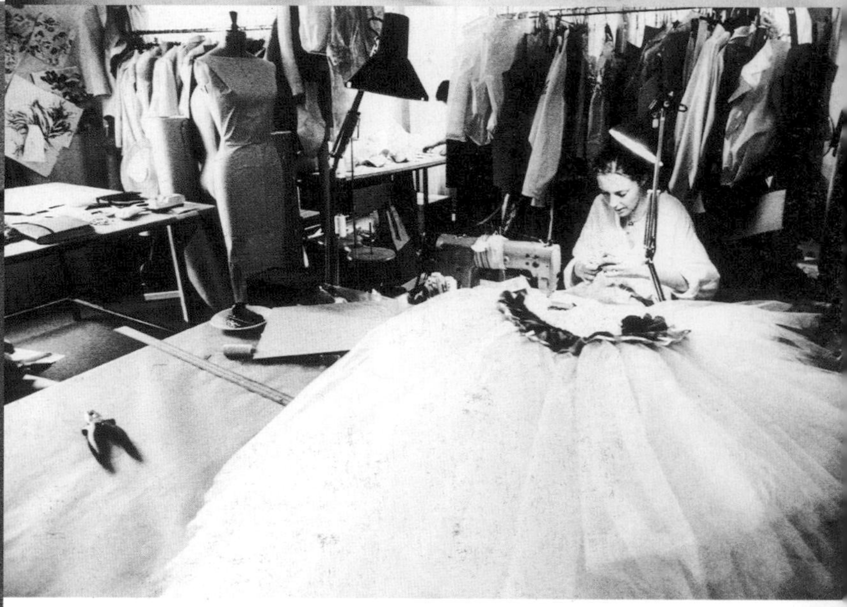

‘Everything is worked out. There is nothing random about a collection.’

II

LONDON:
'The Raw… and the Rarefied'

'When it comes to pressing, I'm the best.'

— JOHN GALLIANO

society must have had a psychological impact. Certainly, life in London dawned raw and hostile for Juan Carlos. Ready for school, he could speak no English. That was traumatic enough, but what the child found hardest to understand was the lack of vibrancy in English life. He remembered the fiestas, with their awe-inspiring emotional power; the bullfights, with their energy and drama. He looked in vain for their equivalent on the grey streets of London. And, for their loss, he found compensation.

Teenage life is difficult for many: for John Galliano it was hell. Teachers at his school found him strange and unfathomable, although not without academic ability. Some worried at his propensity for drawing costume sketches in his school books. Others scoffed. As did his fellow pupils. Beaten by teachers and bullied by boys, he felt a total misfit. 'I thought I was weird. It was only when I'd left that I realized that it was Wilson's Grammar School that was weird.'

He became an introverted, even more shy boy, and increasingly lived in a romantic dream world where, in his imagination, he could re-order history and enjoy the colour and excitement of the past. Surrounded by 'insensitive people, totally out of touch with their feminine sides', it was all that he could do in order to survive. He left school at sixteen, the earliest the law allowed, and moved to City and East London College to study design and printed textiles. It was his lifeline: 'I realized that there were other people in the world like me.'

It was from this background that he went on to St Martin's in order to complete a Foundation Year, an educational course deliberately unconstrained, in order to allow students to experience a wide range of artistic disciplines before deciding which one they would specialize in for their degree. Up to this point, John had toyed with the idea of becoming a fashion illustrator but, in fact, he decided to enrol for the BA course in fashion.

From the start, he loved it. Although he now says 'I kept myself to myself at St Martin's, creatively and socially,' he was noted by his tutors for the way he drew people to him. He was also noted for his absences, especially on Wednesday and Thursday afternoons. They knew him for a hard worker – his tutor, Sheridan Barnett, considered him a workaholic as a student – and assumed he was working at home or in a library somewhere. In fact, he was making money. Desperate to eke out the tiny funds on which he had to live, he obtained a job as a dresser at the National Theatre. And what it gave him was much more valuable and lasting than ready cash.

Working with actors like Sir Ralph Richardson and Nigel Havers on plays as diverse as *The Importance of Being Earnest*, *Major Barbara* and the latest Alan Ayckbourn, he learned to turn his hand at most things

Galliano's deep love of the theatre shows itself in his willingness to dress up and play a part for the camera. It is also a throwback to his student years when whole days were spent in creating outrageous costumes for a weekend's heavy clubbing in London's Soho. (Photo: Paolo Roversi)

No student show has ever had the sheer bravura of John Galliano's 'Incroyables'. Although it lasted less than fifteen minutes it electrified London fashion circles with its wit, originality and confidence. Based on the French revolution, it was supported by sketchbooks showing how clearly post-revolutionary France had influenced him to evolve a completely new approach to cutting clothes.

Right, photos: Niall McInerney, 1984

behind the scenes. 'I was so small, I could get anywhere. In a complicated set, I could be underneath, dressing the actor. I did everything from polishing shoes to opening doors when they had to come off stage. I learned a lot, but the most important thing was pressing. When it comes to pressing, I'm the best. I was famous for it at the National. The actors would insist that they would only have their suits pressed by me.'

He was learning a skill vital to a future couturier. Balenciaga, along with Vionnet the most technically accomplished couturier of the century, believed that everything that mattered in tailoring could be achieved only by the skilful use of the iron to coax and control fabric into behaving as it was required. John learned this basic lesson in the wardrobe of the National Theatre, a place where he was so happy that he says, 'I used to ring up the wardrobe mistress whenever I could see a space and say, "Look, things are a bit slack, can I come and do a couple of weeks for you?"'

It wasn't only to make money, it was because the theatre fired his imagination and taught him something about clothes that was not always apparent away from the heightened world of the stage: 'I used to watch Dame Judi Dench or Zoë Wannamaker in the wings, waiting to go on. I loved them both and I learned so much about a woman and her relationship with her

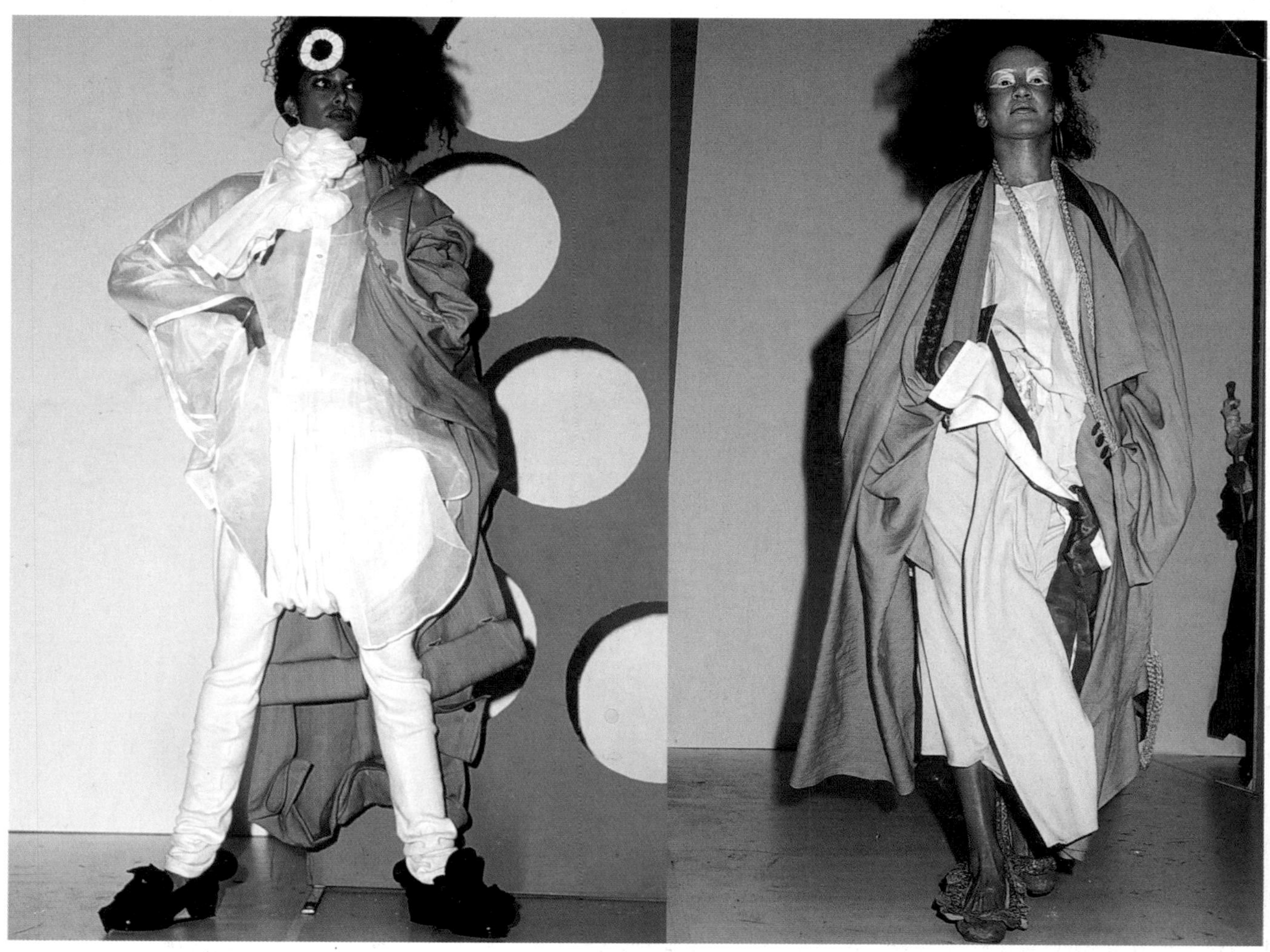

clothes just by watching them.' What he was observing would prove crucial in later years as he began to make theatrical demands on models, persuading them to become performers in order to show his clothes in a completely new way. He watched as the actresses, waiting for their cue, ordered their dress as an essential preliminary to commanding their space – one of the bedrocks of a successful performance.

Even as early as his second year in college, Galliano's intensity was beginning to show. He drew endlessly; he researched not only in the college library but also at the Victoria & Albert Museum; he delved into the more romantic and flamboyant periods of history. Above all, he learned everything he could about the practicalities of clothes-making. He was especially intrigued by the cutter's skills and began to experiment with revolutionary alternatives to standard approaches. Although many of his ideas proved impractical, he had enough success to convince himself that there were other ways to cut a sleeve, or to organize a skirt to fall in a different way.

Looking back, Galliano claims, 'My fashion has been a constant evolution of ideas which I began to explore even before I had left college. I think I knew then that I had a strongly marked road to go down. All that experimental cutting led me to understand precisely how a jacket had been put together in the past; how to put it together correctly in the present and then, from that, I was led to dismantle it and reassemble it in a way that would point to the future. I never saw any

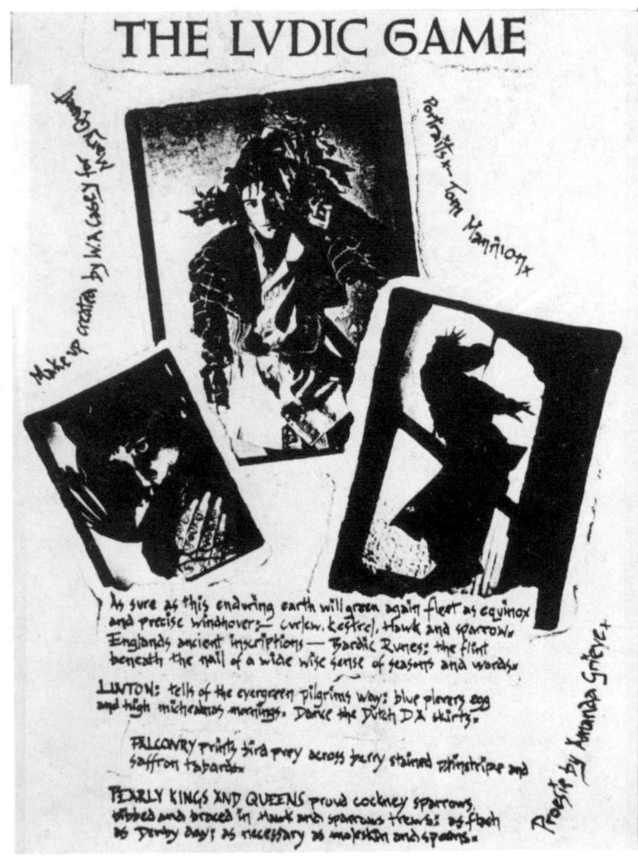

Galliano has always named his collection, often to hauntingly memorable effect. His degree show, 'Les Incroyables', was followed by 'Afghanistan Repudiates Western Ideals', in turn followed by 'The Ludic Game' and 'Forgotten Innocents': they all demonstrated the designer's radical rethinking of fashion in terms of Blake's 'Songs of Innocence and Experience': this was fashion for those previously considered too young for it.

point in stopping at the way in which conventional wisdom decreed a jacket should be cut. Early on, I realized how important it is just to be curious. You mustn't be frightened or hide behind pre-conceived ideas. You *have* to experiment. You just *do* it and it's beautiful because you discover an energy there which feeds you. There are no rules.

Almost as if to prove that, John Galliano set out to discover a theme for his final year, culminating in his degree show, which would bring together the things which he had already learned – the things that mattered to him. He wanted to use the romantic beauty of the costume of the past in a way which would be not merely modern but revolutionary. He wanted to challenge the architecture of fashion – how it is cut, assembled and worn – in order to radically reform opinion on the purpose of dress. He wanted colour, illusion, drama and theatricality. He wanted what he'd

learned at the National, enjoyed in New Romanticism and been excited by in the club scene. More than anything else, he wanted to explore areas not previously examined.

He found what he was searching for in post-revolutionary France, that brief historic period which saw the flowering of fantastic fashion on the backs of disaffected, doomed youth not so very far in spirit from the young London clubbers whose numbers were soon to be cut down by the twin scourges of drug addiction and Aids. There were other similarities. Just as sexual licence and exposure of the body were characteristics of the lunatic fringe of French youth in the 1790s, so permissiveness was confused with progressiveness by their counterparts in early eighties' London. And both groups dressed the part. The New Romantics sprang from the same ideological, social and creative soil as the 'Incroyables', and their female equivalents the 'Merveilleuses', had in the brief period between the collapse of monarchist France in 1792 and the election of Napoleon as Consul for Life in 1802.

Galliano's degree show was notable for the strength and power of his menswear. It broke most of the known rules to produce a triumphantly new look. Unfortunately Galliano no longer designs for men, but many of his ideas have been taken up by others. (Photo: Paolo Roversi)

The essence of the Incroyables movement was misrule. Clothes were used as political and social weapons to show not only a contempt for civilization, but also a disregard for its standards, rules and sensibilities. Exaggeration and deformity were its trademarks. Clothes were slashed and torn; details were grotesquely enlarged; pre-revolutionary dress was parodied. Women wore high-waisted muslin dresses *à la Greque* which left little to the imagination. Men wore huge cravats, high collars and pantaloons, which were cut provocatively tightly in order to emphasize the masculine bulge.

Society was outraged, but the artists and cartoonists loved the look. It was their work which John Galliano discovered in his researches. It was the images of the brothers Carle and Horace Vernet, affectionately capturing the more extreme fashion extravagances, that he began to copy into his notebooks. What he didn't know was that he had lighted on a group with one other similarity to the New Romantics: the Incroyables and Merveilleuses were, like all those who dress to extremes, a tiny group with a minute influence on mainstream late nineteenth-century French fashion. In the same way, New Romanticism remained largely confined to the clubs and the pages of youth-orientated style magazines such as *The Face* and *Arena*.

None of which stopped Galliano's degree show of July 1984 having an impact far beyond the confines of St Martin's School of Art. Nothing so uncompromisingly bold had previously been seen in the work of a student. Nothing had previously linked the romance and theatricality of the past so convincingly with the practicality of the present. Galliano received a first-class honours degree; a star was born and a minor period of French history, distorted and magnified by the glass of time, became part of fashion's currency. The dress designer Roland Klein was one of the outside assessors. He recalls, 'I have assessed many students over the years and, frankly, it is difficult to recall their work. I remember every piece of John Galliano's degree collection. I had never seen a student's work with so much conviction, maturity and technical skill, let alone the originality of his concepts.'

It was, as fashion folk say, a 'moment'. Galliano's clothes were the finale of the student show, the climax of a growing excitement. For days, fellow students had been helping him finish his collection. They had queued up to model it. Their exuberance and

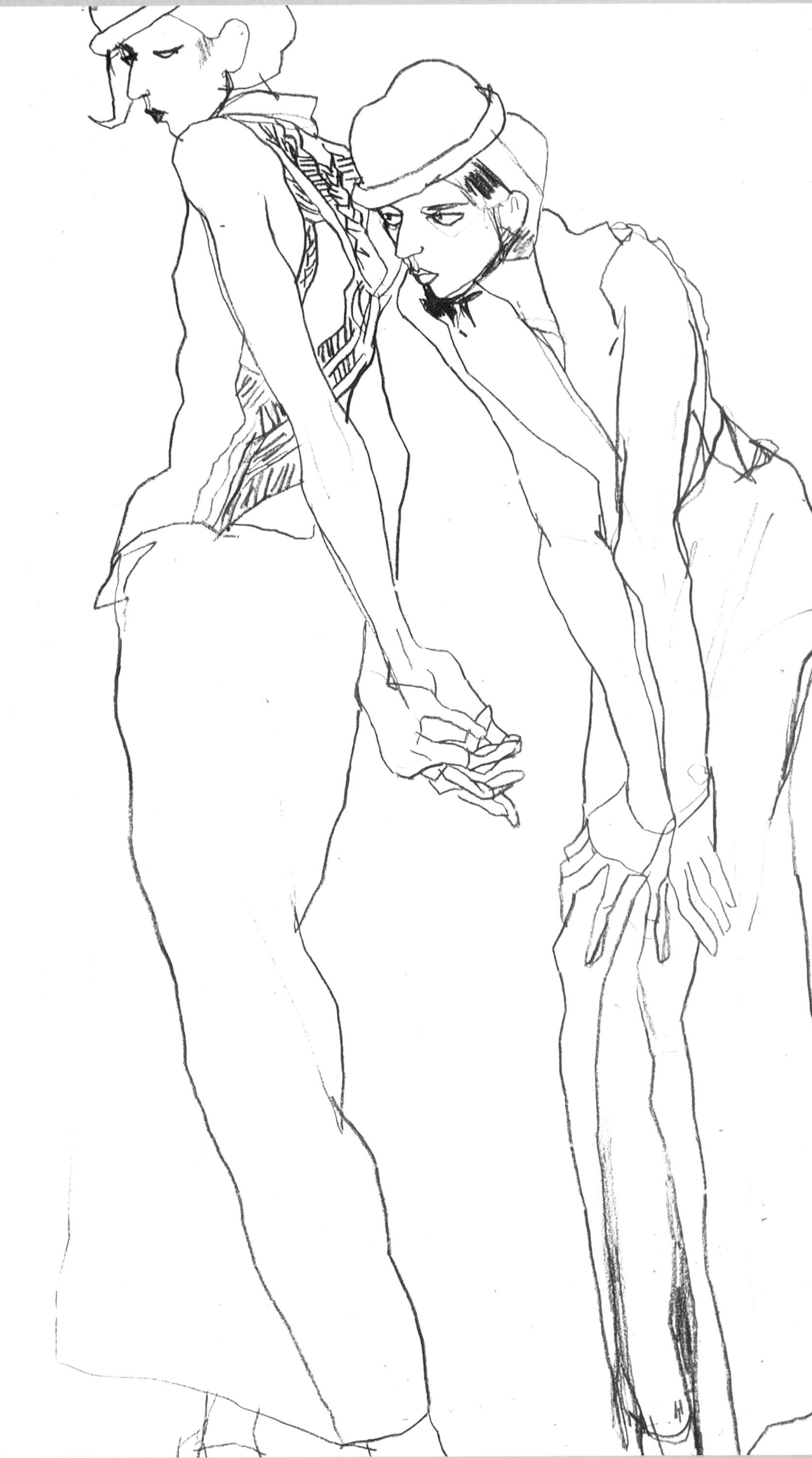

enthusiasm was entirely in keeping with the confidence and wit of the clothes. It was a benchmark show and, even before it had finished, John Galliano had, while still technically a student, become the golden hope of young British fashion, just as David Hockney had for British art in 1962 with his degree show at the Royal College of Art.

Of course, there was hype in both instances. In Galliano's case it was inevitable. The world's eyes were attuned to London fashion which was, in the words of one commentator, 'enjoying one of its frequent fifteen minutes of fame' at all levels, from club scene to salon. It already had its stars. Katharine Hamnett, David Holah and Stevie Stewart of Body Map, Stephen Linard and Vivienne Westwood were all attracting attention by outrageously breaking the rules of fashion, taste and probability. Andrew Logan's Alternative Miss World competitions delighted with their decadence. Clubs like Heaven, the Mud Club and the Beat Route were centres of the wildest new approaches, although Taboo, the best of them all, was not to open for another year. Characters like Boy George and Marilyn; Leigh Bowery and Trojan; or Scarlett Bordello with her shaved head, cupid bow lips and chicken leg earrings, and other creatures from the strange, twilight world of the sexually fluid, were always good for copy. It was a time of outrage and the world was ready for John Galliano's vision.

But not all who sat in the audience for the St Martin's Final Year Show saw Galliano's contribution merely as a continuation of the bread and circuses which London creativity had become to many media commentators. Watching carefully from her front-row seat was Joan Burstein, co-owner of Brown's, the up-

In the 1980s many fashion commentators felt that Galliano's clothes lacked the commerciality essential to sustain a career. They were wrong, as these drawings make clear: every item would be as wearable today as it was then. (Drawing by Howard Tanguy)

Capturing the spirit of a collection is to do with presentation and emphasis. How a garment is accentuated and highlighted enables trained eyes to understand the underlying fashion story of the season. (Photo: Carrie Branovan)

market fashion shop in South Molton Street, a woman renowned for her fashion judgement and her ability to relate to new ideas and movements which leave others baffled. Although the 'Les Incroyables' collection was composed of only eight interchangeable outfits, intended for men and women, she was amazed at Galliano's originality and verve: 'He was St Martin's best-kept secret. He was different, exciting, a free spirit.' She bought the entire collection. And, as if that were not a proof of total conviction, she went one stage further, and filled the prestigious windows of her store with it.

Neither was an act of extravagance or altruism. Joan Burstein does not take a romantic view of fashion: she is a retailer and her motives are practical. In answer to the criticism that she bought Galliano predominantly for his news value she answers, truthfully, 'We sold every piece.' As Sibylle de Saint Phalle, now head of public relations at Givenchy, but for many years one of John's closest collaborators, points out, 'Mrs Burstein was very faithful. She took the first risk. For a business woman to have the courage of her feelings to the extent that she would back a student with the conviction with which she backed John is very rare and totally admirable. She was always behind him.'

John remembers the weeks that followed as some of the most exciting of his life. 'Mrs Burstein decided on window displays when she saw the collection on the hangers, a while after the show. She invited me to do the windows and help with the selling. Initially what sold were the organdie shirts and the waistcoats. As it all coincided with my parents going on holiday, I was able to take over the house. The front room became a mini factory. There was a machine in there and we made up the clothes as the orders came through. I'd go to Notting Hill and buy old curtains and brocades; cart them home and then my friends would come in to help cut them. It was a sort of perfect cottage industry. We'd produce, deliver, get some money up front and then start the process over. Looking back, it was so amateur it had to change but, God, it was fun. Mrs B. was marvellous. She let me meet customers and did everything she could to help me reach a wider audience. It really was a very pure form of patronage and I'll never forget what she did for me.'

The buzz surrounding John Galliano in London fashion circles was growing louder, and interest in his work was spreading beyond South Molton Street. 'I remember walking past Joseph with some friends and one of them stopped at one of the windows. "Here!" she said, "They're your waistcoats. He's ripped you off!" I was quite flattered. It seemed rather special to be ripped off when you'd only just left college a few weeks but, in fact my friend was wrong. Joseph had seen them in Brown's and was so eager to have them in his shop he had bought them retail from Mrs B. And he was another one who was incredibly supportive.'

As was Amanda Grieve (now Amanda Harlech), working at that time as a stylist on *Harpers and Queen*. Like Mrs Burstein she had found John's show an explosion of imaginative ideas and radical thinking. She met him, they got on like brother and sister almost immediately and became friends and colleagues who were destined to work closely with each other for the next eleven years. She remembers the thrill of finding another person so attuned to her way of thinking that 'he finishes off your sentences for you. I loved his passion and self-belief, right from the beginning. Even then – and this really isn't hindsight – I knew he was fortune's child. I had a sense of being drawn compulsively to John and his creativity – I knew I had to work with him.' She was styling the cover for Malcolm McLaren's LP *Fans* and she asked John to help her. Even now, he looks back and considers it one of his 'moments'. He loved working with McLaren and Amanda. They came up not with a costume, but with an enormous fan covered with strips of Chinese newspaper for a naked 'Madam Butterfly' to hide behind.

John was beginning to make contacts who would stay with him for many years, always working for little money – and often for no money at all. They didn't mind because they knew that John was even poorer than they were. He admits, 'I was a club demon. I think everybody knows by now. Music is vital to me and, in the mid-eighties, there was only one place to be. Taboo was the best.' Founded by Leigh Bowery and his friend Trojan, it so caught the frenetic mood of young London in the mid-eighties that everybody creative had to go there. Once described as an early Groucho club, but with spirit, it was much more, surpassing the Dean Street den of media folk as a place to both pose and be pretentious. As Bowery told *LAM* magazine, 'The name's a joke really. There's nothing you can't do there.'

'The club scene fed me,' John says. 'Being with other creative people like Boy George was a crucial experience to me. That's where I first met Stephen Jones, the milliner, although I'd heard of his reputation from St Martin's. Sibylle, who was later to work with me, was his assistant and so I approached him about making hats: "Please, please, will you do my show for me?"' He laughs. 'He was terribly grand, gave me that "No time for *you* sweetheart" look and that was *that*. Of course, he was doing the business then, making

There has often been a soulful beauty in John Galliano's heroines. They seem to live in a world different from the commercial and they are seen by many as beyond the reality of fashion. Their ethereal quality is enhanced by clothes which float and glide around their bodies to create a timeless romanticism. (Model, Marie-Sophie Wilson, photo: Xavier von Valhonrat)

By the late 1980s, deceptively simple shapes based on highly complex cutting techniques had become part of the Galliano design lexicon. He was a bold experimenter, pushing his techniques way beyond the line which many of his contemporaries would have feared to cross. (Photo: Galliano archives)

hats for Comme des Garçons and Montana. No time for little runts straight out of St Martin's!' In fact, Stephen Jones did eventually start to make hats for John Galliano, and it is a creative partnership which has worked extremely well. As John says, 'I love him because, apart from being so creative, he is *very* professional and businesslike – the sort of person who is passionate about every part of his job. That's what I like.'

The post Incroyables euphoria couldn't last for ever. A front room is not a sustainable base for a fashion career. Galliano needed a backer. He appeared in the form of Johan Brun (known affectionately to John and his friends as Yo-Yo), who had seen John's clothes in Brown's window. 'He was a very young entrepreneur,' John remembers. 'He said, "I want to order but I also want to manage you." We went for a few drinks together and we were clearly on the same wavelength. He asked me what I was doing and I explained the problem: "I've nowhere to work and no money to buy fabrics, but the good thing is that the shops want my clothes."' Johan found a space in a run-down building in Earl Street, just off Finsbury Park in north London. 'It was grotty but at least it was a place. We rented a small area in a studio belonging to a photographer – near the sink. So there I was, dyeing fabric, hanging it out to dry, ironing, cutting, making it up. All very *ad hoc*. Mates came in and helped where they could. It was great.' Amanda Grieve recalls it as 'a beautiful loft-like space, high up, overlooking Liverpool Street station, always full of marvellous people. Everybody came to see John there, from Boy George to Mr Francis, who made the most marvellous silk flowers in London.'

They were working towards 'Afghanistan Repudiates Western Ideals'. Not a fashion show, it was a static display mounted as a stand, part of London Fashion Week at Olympia, and can be seen now as less a collection than a statement of intent – or even a warning shot fired across the bows of the fashion establishment. In political terms and attitude, Galliano stood as entirely his own man. He was more. His approach, radical and uncompromising, showed attitudes to dress, life and culture sharply at variance with the canons of accepted London fashion approaches. The impact of 'Afghanistan Repudiates ...' rested not only with the fundamental re-thinking of the nature of dress which the pieces exemplified, but also with the fact that, beyond the overt political commentary of the title, there were layers of social and sartorial subversion.

The title, and inspiration, came from an arcane moment in history when King Amanullah Khan, who ruled Afghanistan from 1919 to 1929, issued a decree three years into his reign forbidding his subjects from wearing national costume and requiring them to dress in Western fashions. His attempts at sumptuary control, like those in Europe and America from the fourteenth to the seventeenth centuries, failed, and he was deposed. What stimulated Galliano was the idea of the people of Afghanistan trying to comply. As he told the *Daily News Record*, 'I like the idea of the tension and romance of wearing two different cultures.'

It was a collection of remarkable originality and maturity of vision for a designer who had been out of college only four months. Mixing ethnic shapes with standard British tailoring, he explained to *The Face*, 'I love the hip. My tops are baggy at the back, tight at the waist and loosing downwards after that ... The idea for this collection came from a cartoon I saw in a thirties edition of *Punch* ... servants and gentlemen robed in smart European dress. Just like all the Indians

John
Galliano

The John Galliano logo, a modest, even amateur affair, was stamped on the forehead of the models in 'Forgotten Innocents'. For the final entrance water poured over it caused it to run in an unsettling, anarchic fashion, making the girls seem victims of some unspoken violation – an approach which was to be taken up by many designers in future years. (Photos: left, of Sybille de St Phalle, by Michael Woolley; right and far right: Niall McInerney)

classic Galliano touch, referring to the epidemic of 'Muslin Disease', that struck Paris in 1803, when women died of influenza because they immersed themselves in water before going out so that their clothes would cling to them like those in Greek sculpture. It was an ideological gesture in post-revolutionary France which had turned to the cradle of democracy in its attempts to reform society on egalitarian terms.

For Galliano, it was about purity: 'It was all to do with deconstruction. Removing the mystique and showing the reality. I piped the seams on the outside with gaffer tape.' It was also about fundamentally re-examining preconceptions – a line of investigation he took further in his next collection, 'Forgotten Innocents'. Amanda Harlech recalls it as 'a very beautiful show put together under duress... no money... it was about seeing things as a child might. Pick up a spoon, strip away your preconceptions and it becomes a wondrous object. Forgotten Innocents was about that.' Galliano adds, 'It was about alternative ways of putting clothes together. I was experimenting with circular cutting, which causes wonderful stress to fabric, and attenuated drapes, but without tucking. I got the idea from Savile Row and how tailors cut sleeves to swing forward. We just exaggerated it by pushing it as far as it could go. It was an exercise in experimental cutting and breaking down preconceived ideas of how things could be worn – a bit like little children with a dressing-up box shovelling clothes on anyhow.'

The show opened with Sibylle, hair down to her ankles, knitting a 'cat's cradle' out of wool. Like all the

Scale, cut and volume are infinitely more important to serious designers than is pattern. As the drawings show, whether in toile (left) or finished form (right), conviction is what brings the power which makes a garment memorable. (Drawings by Howard Tanguy)

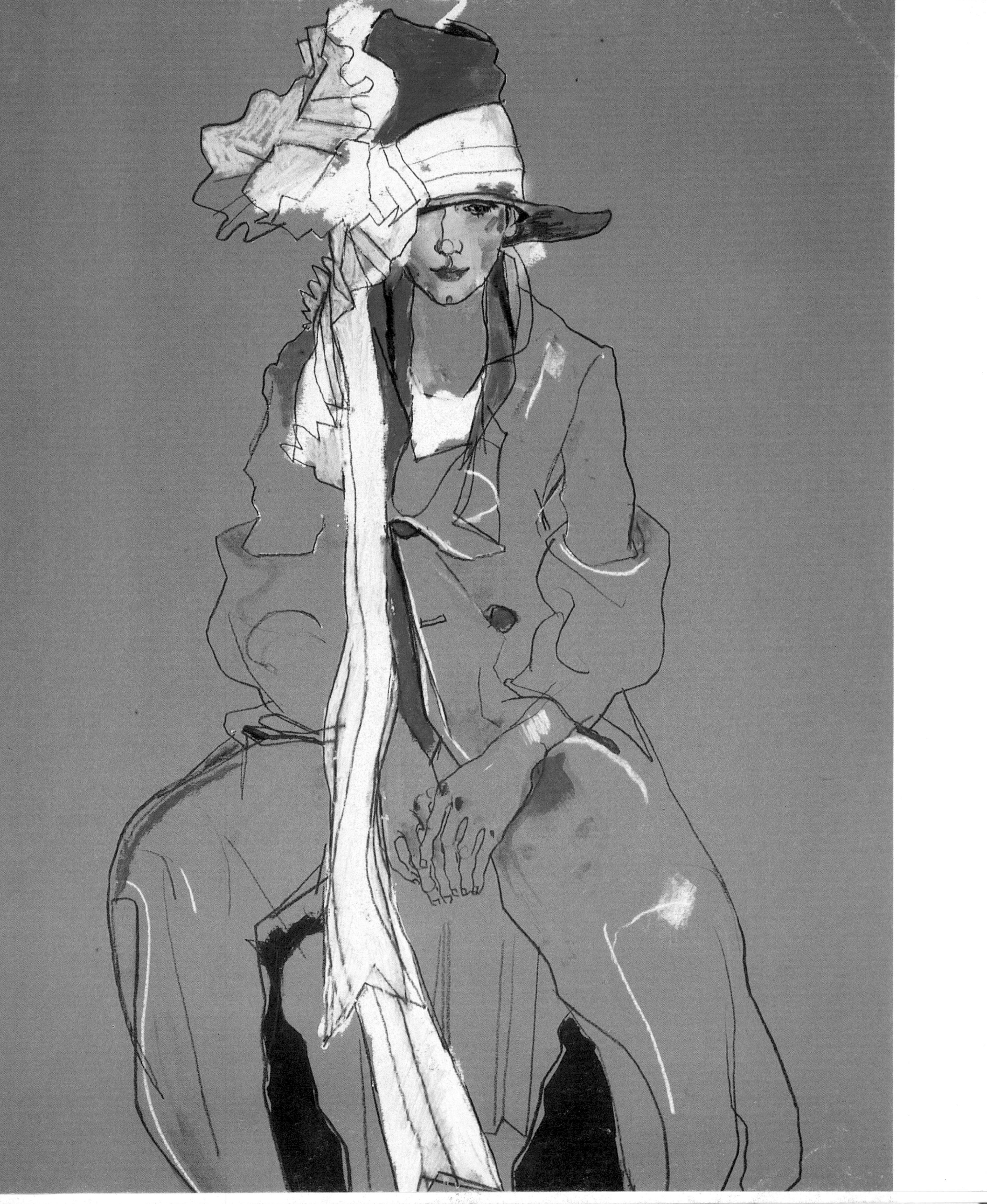

‘Curiosity: it’s the most important thing.’

III

INSPIRATIONS: Themes and Variations

DO WE CRITICIZE STOCKHAUSEN for his failure to produce tunes which might be whistled in the street? Is Willem de Kooning to be condemned because his images cannot sit comfortably on suburban walls? Are Ezra Pound's words rejected because they lack the accessibility of an advertising jingle? Trailblazers are expected to step slightly ahead of the world, opening up possibilities and formulating challenges with which we later catch up.

The same is true of fashion leaders. Their job is not to present us with clothes barely distinguishable from those currently available in the high street. Their role is to shock, stimulate, excite and amuse. Above all, they should ruffle our complacency by questioning not only our attitudes to beauty, femininity and allure, but also to ourselves.

Great painters, musicians and poets take little notice of what might please the public. They are driven by their belief that they can speak with a creative voice unlike that of anyone else. In fact, this belief in his personal uniqueness is what distinguishes the true artist from the commercial artist whose success depends on singing songs conceived by others and being paid to do so.

To interest a designer, movie stars don't merely have to be glamorous or beautiful. What is important is their personality and the strength it brings to their screen portrayals. Both Marlene Dietrich and Gloria Swanson were rich in character as well as looks – which is why they appear in Galliano's sourcebooks.

Previous page: photo by Lauren van der Stockt, Christian Dior archive.

To "the Blue Book
of the Screen"
most sincerely
Gloria

Arrogance – of the intellectual and artistic, rather than the social kind – is the prerogative of the great designer, just as much as it is of the creators in more legitimate and acceptable creative fields. Worth set the standard in the last century. As couturier to the Empress Eugénie and the ladies of virtually every country in Europe, he knew how women should dress, and any who dared to question his judgement were instantly dismissed his salon and allowed no possibility of re-entry, regardless of power or petulance. Paul Poiret, who in the twenties was the first couturier to create a perfume bearing his name, was a total autocrat. His autobiography rings with edicts beginning, 'I decided… ', and even, 'I decreed …' Chanel, although cannily interested in making money, was content only to lead, never to follow, the women of an infinitely higher social class with whom she mixed. Balenciaga, the most austere and creatively arrogant of all twentieth-century designers, was asked to put his name to certain goods to be manufactured under licence, at huge personal profit. He refused to compromise his integrity for something as transient as money. It is this inability to compromise – not out of pig-headedness as much from sheer incomprehension of any other vision than their own – that puts certain dress designers on the level of the artist.

John Galliano joins them, for the same reason. Nobody can pretend that Galliano's career has been smooth-flowing. Though he may graze the Elysian fields now, the fashion world has been prepared to see him face ruin in the past, capable of doing little more than beating its collective breast and saying, 'Poor John. A genius – but so uncommercial.' As a judgement, it is as arrogant as it is misinformed; a knee-jerk, unthinking reaction; a blatant piece of guilt-transference, a refusal to face the facts of the man's career.

Galliano's impact on the fashion industry, apparent even in his first show, should have been electric. It wasn't. Instead, it was ignored. Journalists became excited, retailers were interested, but the industry itself – the manufacturers, chief design executives and financiers, sitting on a moribund structure which, in real terms had hardly moved forward for a hundred years – was too lazy, complacent, and involved with making instant, easy profits to address the Galliano challenge. 'Impossible to put into production,' the pundits said, while admiring the radical new approach he was suggesting.

They were right. Galliano's cut was quite impossible to mass-produce using *existing* technical knowledge and experience. But the failure of the industry – and it failed itself as much as it failed Galliano – was to leave it at that point. Nobody was courageous and forward-thinking enough to realize the challenge and address it by finding techniques which would make it possible to manufacture such exciting clothes for a mass market perfectly ready for them. Instead of saying, 'Here is the future, we must find a way of making it possible,' a whole industry turned its back and maintained a manufacturing stasis.

The results we all know. John Galliano was the most forward-thinking and original menswear designer of the century. His clothes from the mid-eighties still look sparklingly modern, attractive and wearable – by a wide range of age groups – and yet he was forced to abandon menswear when he was backed by Aguecheek. His endless requests to include at least some men's designs in his collections were rejected as a self-indulgence. The denial was akin to cutting one of his creative veins, in a spurious blood-letting in order to make him think more 'commercially' – for which we can read 'prosaically'.

The same could be said for Galliano's female fashion. It became too easy to dub him an impractical dreamer, on his own plane, beyond help, rather than finding ways of manufacturing his clothes as he wished them to be made. He was ahead of the pack, but he wasn't that far ahead. Even now, with his name apparently secure, and his reputation as the only new designer of true stature to have emerged since Yves Saint Laurent freely acknowledged, there is still a feeling that Galliano creates clothes merely to gratify his fantasy world.

In fact, Galliano's triumph is a constant reproach to an industry too complacent to take up the challenge he has undoubtedly presented ever since his first collection. But, if the integrity of the fashion industry can be questioned, Galliano's integrity is beyond doubt. Like Chanel and Balenciaga before him, he has a handwriting unmistakably his own and undeviatingly modern. His last ready-to-wear collection, with a strong Chinese bias, demonstrated all his strengths and earned him the sobriquet of the 'Gypsy Rose Lee of Fashion' from *Women's Wear Daily* because he is 'a master of theatre, a master of fantasy. Most importantly, he's a master of making women look beautiful.'

The New York Times, reviewing his Christian Dior ready-to-wear collection, took the opportunity to add its accolade: 'Despite pale imitations that keep springing up, no one could mistake Mr Galliano's design for that of another hand. At Christian Dior, much of the wrenching beauty of Mr Galliano's clothes was in the dramatic styling that his team has perfected beyond compare… with an unmatched understanding of what makes women romantically sexy and beautiful.' Such encomiums are not lightly given but, for Galliano, they are not new. The disgrace of the fashion industry is that John Galliano has been rated extravagantly high since the beginning and yet his challenge was seen as too great to be taken up at manufacturing level.

Many will say that the practicality of John Galliano's work is its least important feature. Certainly, it is a point of view worthy of contemplation. But John Galliano would reject it. For him, a show, vital as it is, is a figurehead for a ship which is entirely commercial. He would claim that, without its ship, a show – no matter how magnificent – becomes an empty thing, a façade, a meaningless piece of decorative trivia, rather like the figureheads from old sailing ships found in cleaned-up, sanitized, theme-park ports and harbours. Galliano's ship currently consists of ten collections, eight of them for Dior. The clothes shown to the press in ready-to-wear and couture are less than a quarter of the total output. It is because three-quarters of his designs are primarily for production that talk of his uncommercial and impractical approach irritates him.

Galliano tells a story from his early days, concerning his fabrication. Tired of trying to buy fabric from London wholesalers, he decided to go to the north of England to source his own fabric supplies. 'We went all over Yorkshire, visiting mills where they had marvellous unwashed wools with no silicone finishes. Although I had no money, I was excited by experimental fabrics, even then. One I'll never forget was called Linton tweed. It was green and black with a mohair overcheck. It looked as if a sheep had caught its fleece on barbed wire. I loved using it.' The same practical

'He adores women. That's why he always needs the close presence of a woman in his intimate team.'

– MANOLO BLAHNIK

and directly confrontational approach to production has been the unknown but vital other side to the glitteringly extravagant Galliano coin throughout his career.

Just as the great artists of the past ground their own pigments and prepared their own surfaces before allowing their brushes to be carried away by their imaginations, so a great couturier must have a balance between his creative and practical side, if he is to survive. Fantasy which is not realizable is as sterile as practicality with no imagination. All of the great couturiers have been technicians – although only Chanel and Balenciaga could cut and sew as well as the top hands in their ateliers – as much as they have been artists. Indeed, there are many fashion commentators who insist that creating clothes is much more a craft than an art.

They are wrong, while appearing to be right. At any one time, the number of supreme exponents is small; the number of the competent but inspired is considerable. For one Chanel, there were hundreds of dressmakers in Paris who stood out above the thousands more that clustered there in obscurity in the thirties. Who but the most arcane specialist now recalls Bruyère, Lafaurie, Nicole Groult or Agnès-Drécoll, all of whom kept quite sizeable and very chic Parisian establishments and were regularly featured in *Vogue*, *L'Officiel*, *Femina* and *Le Jardin des Modes*? And does it matter that their names are lost? Chanel and others of the time, such as Schiaparelli and Molyneux, give validity to what the rest were achieving, but they alone rose above the crowd and, in their rising, put fashion on a different plane.

Still today, in the hands of the majority of practitioners fashion struggles to be accepted as even a minor art. It exists in a strange, twilit landscape, a staging post between high art and high camp, with a little of this, a little of that and lot of what the fashion world itself calls 'rock and roll' – a mixture part-Disneyland, part-Hollywood B-movie, with more than a dash of emotional self-indulgence. It's a world which those outside find hard to take seriously; a world which often has difficulty in separating the meretricious from the worthwhile; a world where the romance of the fight against justice attracts people to the theatricality of Byron more readily than the pragmatism of Garibaldi; a world of taste which prefers its décor designed at second hand by Nancy Cunard or Elsie de Wolfe rather than the Adam brothers or Chippendale.

But it is a world which occasionally throws up people who transcend its tawdriness, people who remind us that good fashion is like good art –

The sophistication of perfect purity of line has always been understood by Galliano. Like Captain Molyneux – a British designer who also moved to Paris to make his name, and who became an icon for Christian Dior – Galliano constantly returns to this concept of 1930s understatement, as he did with this bias-cut dress for his 1994 collection. (Photo: Paolo Roversi)

CLOSE-UP: Creating the Show

ALTHOUGH THEY ARE PROBABLY the most sought-after invitations in the entire fashion world, not all fashion writers and buyers are convinced of the validity of John Galliano's unique and idiosyncratic way of styling his clothes for their first presentation to the world. Those who see clothes as entirely practical artefacts of modern life are uneasy about what they judge to be a wilfully whimsical approach – and their unease begins with the invitation.

Invitations to John Galliano fashion shows are unlike any others. Carefully judged to capture both the mood of the clothes and their presentation, they give much more information than mere venue and time. Essentially, they are the first romantic contact between couturier and audience: an invitation to suspend disbelief and to enter Galliano's world on Galliano's terms. Above all, they are a declaration of intent.

An invitation to a Galliano fashion show is no pedestrian thing. As much effort goes into it as any other aspect of a presentation because he knows that this is his opportunity to convey the spirit which captures the imagination even before the first dress has appeared. (Photo: Andrew McPherson)

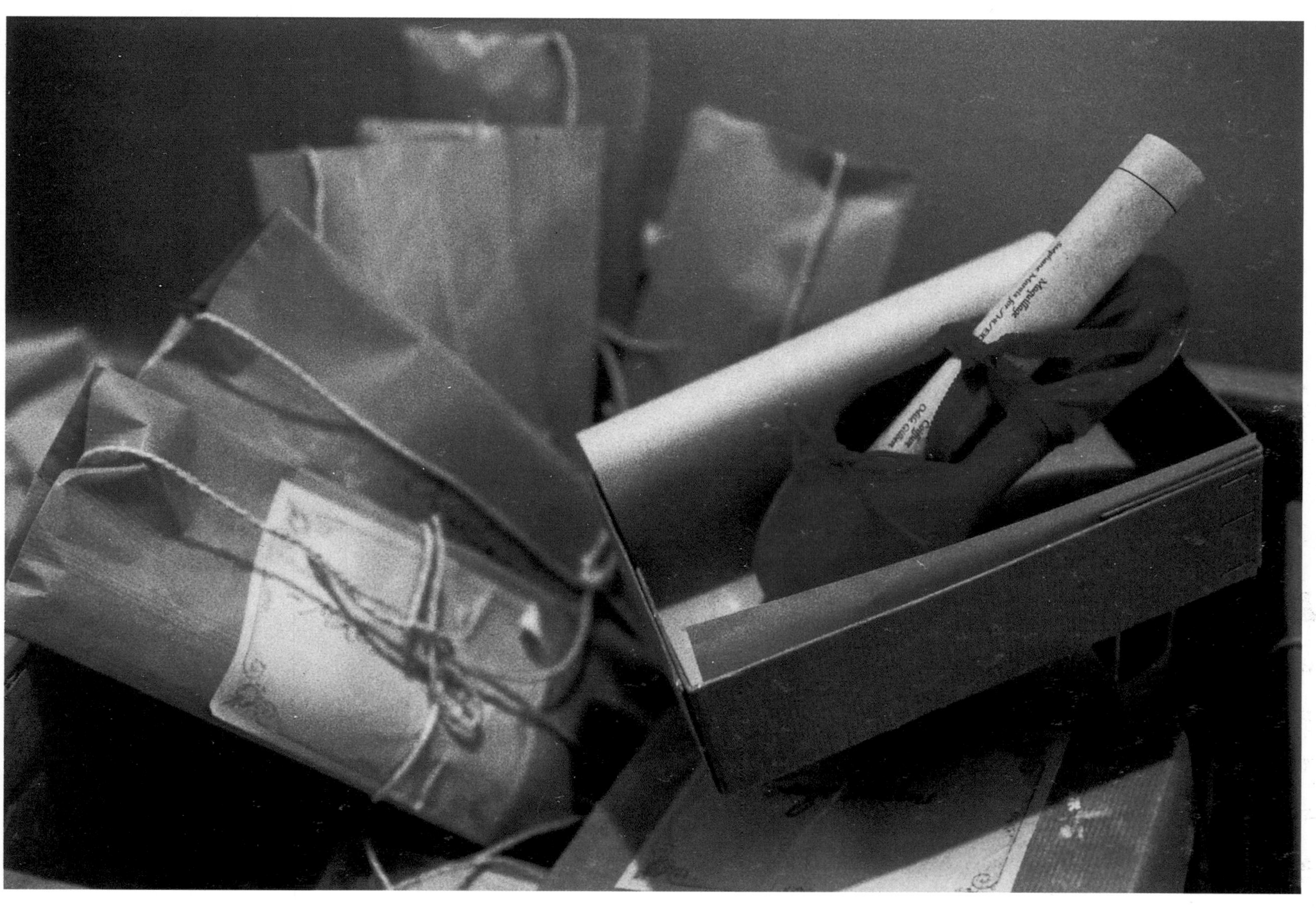

An amateur boxing promotional hand-out from the twenties; a Russian doll containing a silver charm bracelet; some desert sand, a bullet and a cache of love letters; a ruby-red ballet slipper and a rose; a hastily written telegram, a rusty key with a handwritten label; even a fifties style school report – such things can infuriate as much as delight. But nobody throws these invitations away, no matter how much they may be irritated by what they see as a fey refusal to come to terms with the real world. And the reason they don't is simple: love it, or hate it, a John Galliano show – either for his own name collection or for Christian Dior – is an unmissable experience.

It is also challengingly different from any other shows, and takes weeks of involvement from John and his team, who see it as a much more positive and creative thing than merely the vehicle for showing clothes. To them, it is integral to the whole concept of the clothes, in the way that a Renaissance frame is to a picture or a jeweller's setting is for a gem: the one loses something without the other. John Galliano would go further and say the one is seriously weakened without the other. In his mind, the clothes and their presentation are indivisible.

For those who haven't witnessed a Galliano presentation, it is important to know what it is – and

Creating the mood of a John Galliano show depends on conjuring the right atmosphere in the venue. Much work and planning goes into the mise en scène, *whether it is in order to create a peasant circus, the downtown area of an American city in the fifties or a Hollywood film set in the thirties.*

is not. To begin with, it is meant to be an intimate, interactive occasion for a severely limited number of guests. Most French shows expect to seat well over a thousand people with many guests standing; a Galliano own-name show is limited to 500-odd seats with, officially at least, no guests standing. Traditional runway shows have banks of seating ranged on either side of the raised runway, placing press on one side and buyers on the other. The prime position, reserved for the top journalists, VIPs and photographers, who stand behind them, is at the end of the runway. The seating is hierarchical and divisive. Depending on the designer, and how he and his press and PR staff rate individuals, publications, stores and manufacturers, everyone is seated according to status, power, buying and publicity clout and, although most are happy with their placing, there are inevitably mistakes ending in ruffled *amour propre*.

Galliano's approach avoids such pitfalls. Eschewing the angular, raised runway as being too constraining, he chooses venues which allow his models to stroll a serpentine line through several rooms. Whereas in a traditional show the climactic moments are when the models reach the end of the runway, in a Galliano presentation there are many different moments. As his press officer, Mesh Chhibber explains, 'John feels that

it is very important to create a sympathetic atmosphere. He insists that as many guests as possible should have a good view. We have as many front row seats as possible by lengthening the distance, stringing it out through several rooms. He also breaks down the audience barriers. He won't have press all blocked together in one place, and buyers in another. He mixes them, and the nationalities. The only thing he insists upon is practical: writers for newspapers must have good seats because, unlike the rest of the audience, they usually have to turn around their copy immediately. They don't have time to come to the showroom and examine the clothes, so they must have an uninterrupted view that enables them to see everything at the show.'

Mesh maintains that the Galliano system makes his life easier because there is no one prestigious room in which all the guests feel they have a right to be. All rooms through which the models pass have their own *mise en scène* with their moments of drama and excitement worked out and created by John and the team. When they have decided where the key point of each room is to be, the photographers are placed accordingly. They are crucial to how the room is to be

Amanda Harlech was for many years involved with creating the atmosphere of a show with John Galliano. Her notebooks are a vivid chronicle of two minds steadfastly following one creative path, crammed as they are with notes, sketches, polaroids and swatches of material.

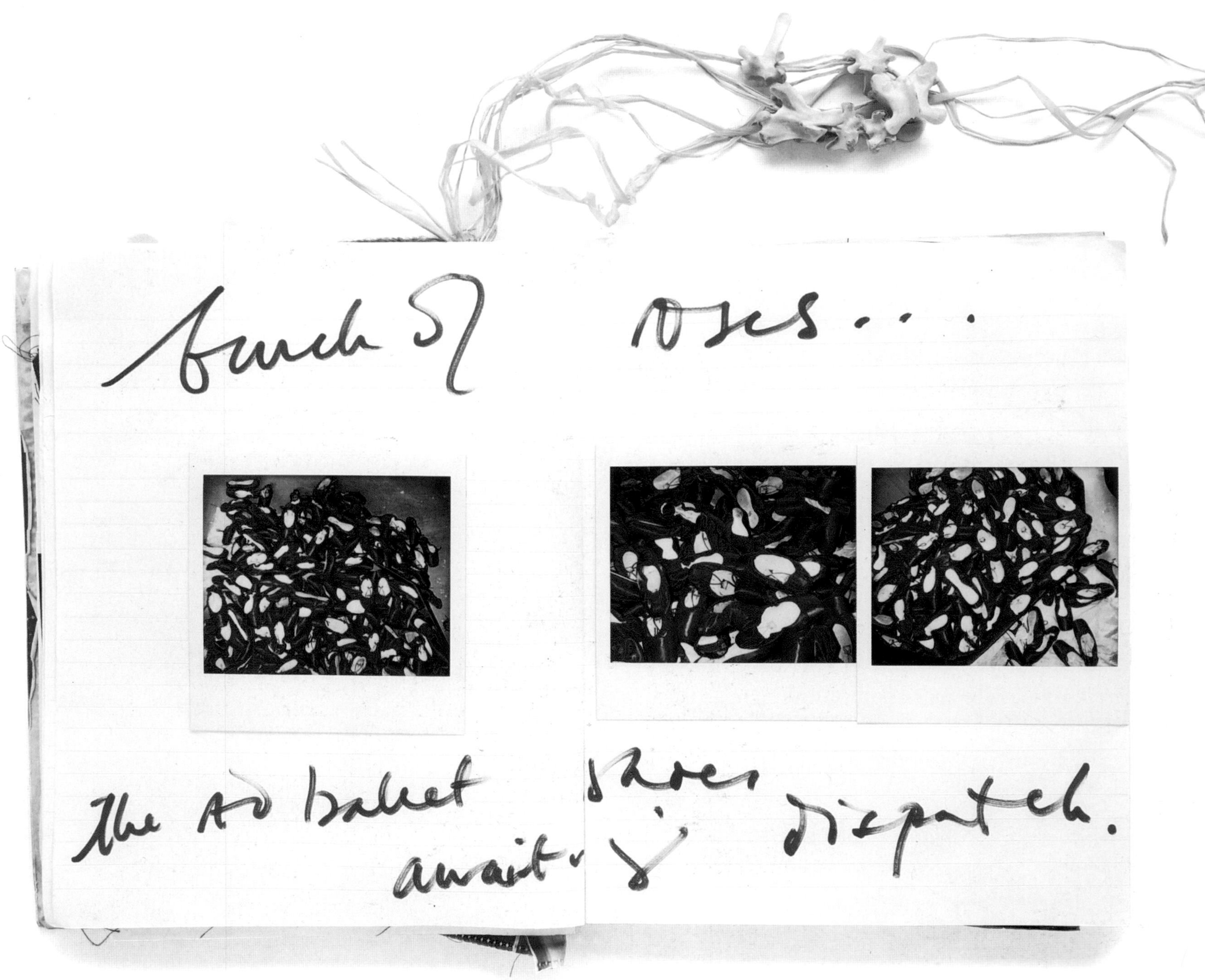

'worked' because they give the models a focal point to which they can act. As John says, 'There is nothing random about the show. It is all carefully planned, like a film. And the venue and how it is to be is decided early on – in tandem with the clothes, really. In other words, as we are designing the clothes, we are thinking not only how they will work together but also how they will work within the story. How they will help to *tell* the story.'

As with a film set, the dressing of the venue is vitally important. The set designer with whom John prefers to work is Jean-Luc Ardouin, who might be asked to create a rooftop scene, a gypsy circus, or even, as he did for the Galliano Autumn–Winter 1997 collection, shown in the Musée Nationale des Monuments Français in the Palais de Chaillot in March 1997, a Cecil B. de Mille-style film set. The props required are always considerable, but for the 'Suzy Sphinx' show, as it was known, the demands were formidable. Suzy, the heroine, was taken from an English girl's school, through Egypt to Hollywood, where she ended up playing Cleopatra in a film. A story-line rich with ironies required a setting with the same mood. The props not only had to be authentic, they also required

a camp quality that would send up the kitsch atmosphere of Hollywood B-movies without allowing the humour to undermine the magnificence. So, along with peacock thrones, obelisks, fallen Egyptian masonry inscribed with hieroglyphics, sand, rich fabrics, pottery and copper, there was film lighting, camera bogies and their railway tracks, all skillfully mixed to stimulate the audience imagination and make it receptive to the overall tale even before a model appeared.

In order to create such elaborate sets, it is not merely money and hard graft that are required. The venue, once chosen, must be passed as safe with both the fire and security authorities. 'The *préfecture* of police liaise with us through the show specialists,' Mesh says. 'The regulations about numbers and safety are much more stringent in Paris than in London. For example, no one is allowed to be more than fifty yards from a fire exit, which clearly dictates the décor and how each room and its seating may be laid out.' Steven Robinson adds, 'Dressing a set is a long process of trial and error. It can take weeks to find the perfect Empire chair. When Amanda was a part of the team she used to take on a lot of the responsibility, because she always knew how to interpret what John wanted it to be.' John agrees. 'She was marvellous at making things look as if they'd just casually come together, almost by accident, but it takes an incredible amount of time and determination to get everything right.'

The set takes three days to assemble and dress, and John checks everything, working as a stage director. Every night – sometimes it is well past midnight if fittings have been complicated and time-consuming – he goes to the venue – where everyone is still working – to check that the day's work has fulfilled his brief. Invariably, there are adjustments to be made: 'That lighting is too bright' – Galliano uses theatrical rather than runway lighting – or 'That yellow is too strong' – clearly, all colours are chosen to complement the fabric

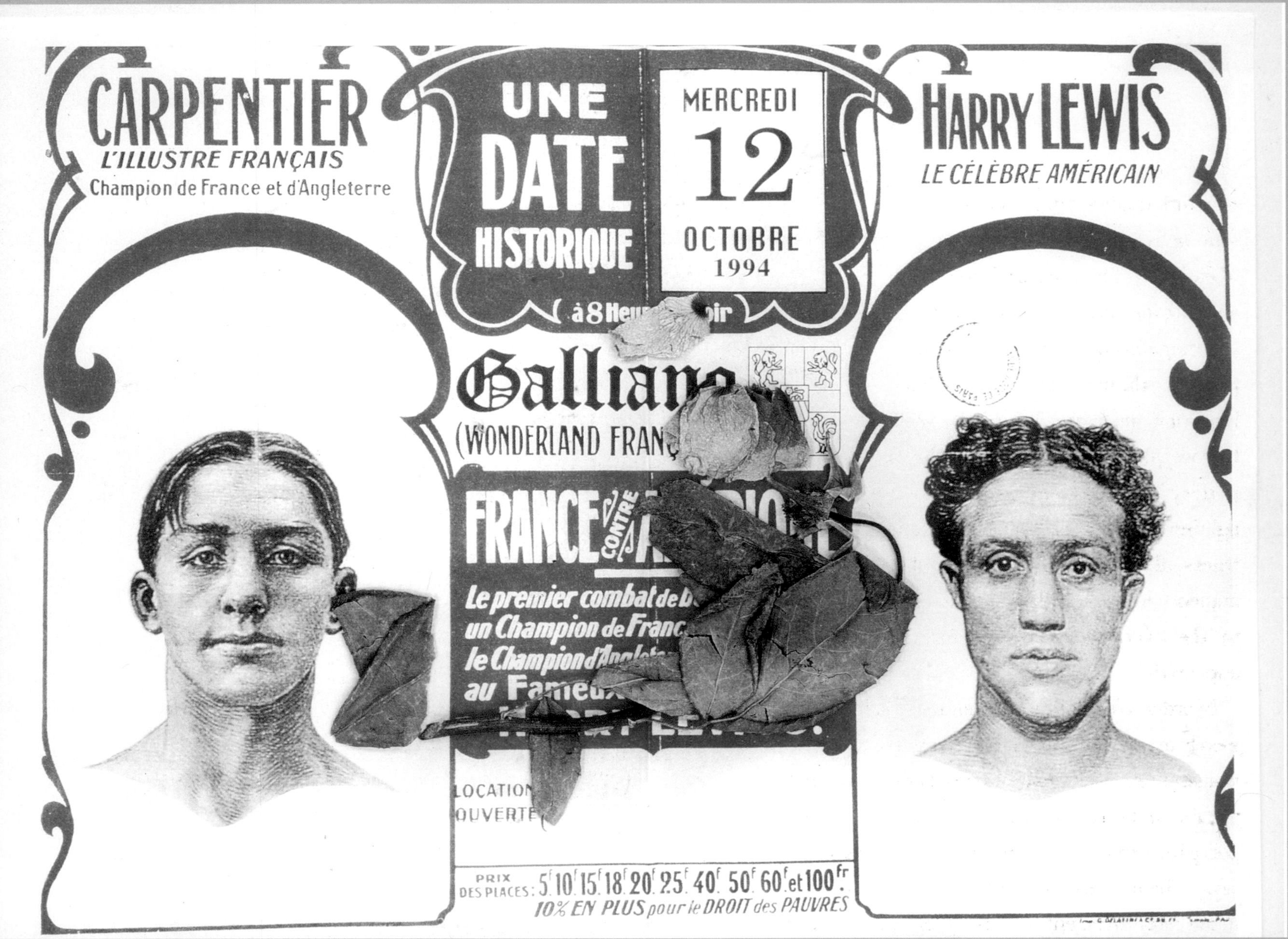

School reports, boxing promotional hand-outs, Russian boxes and (overleaf) telegrams, desert sand and bullets have all been used as invitations to Galliano shows. For true fashion followers, they are collector's items from the moment they are received.

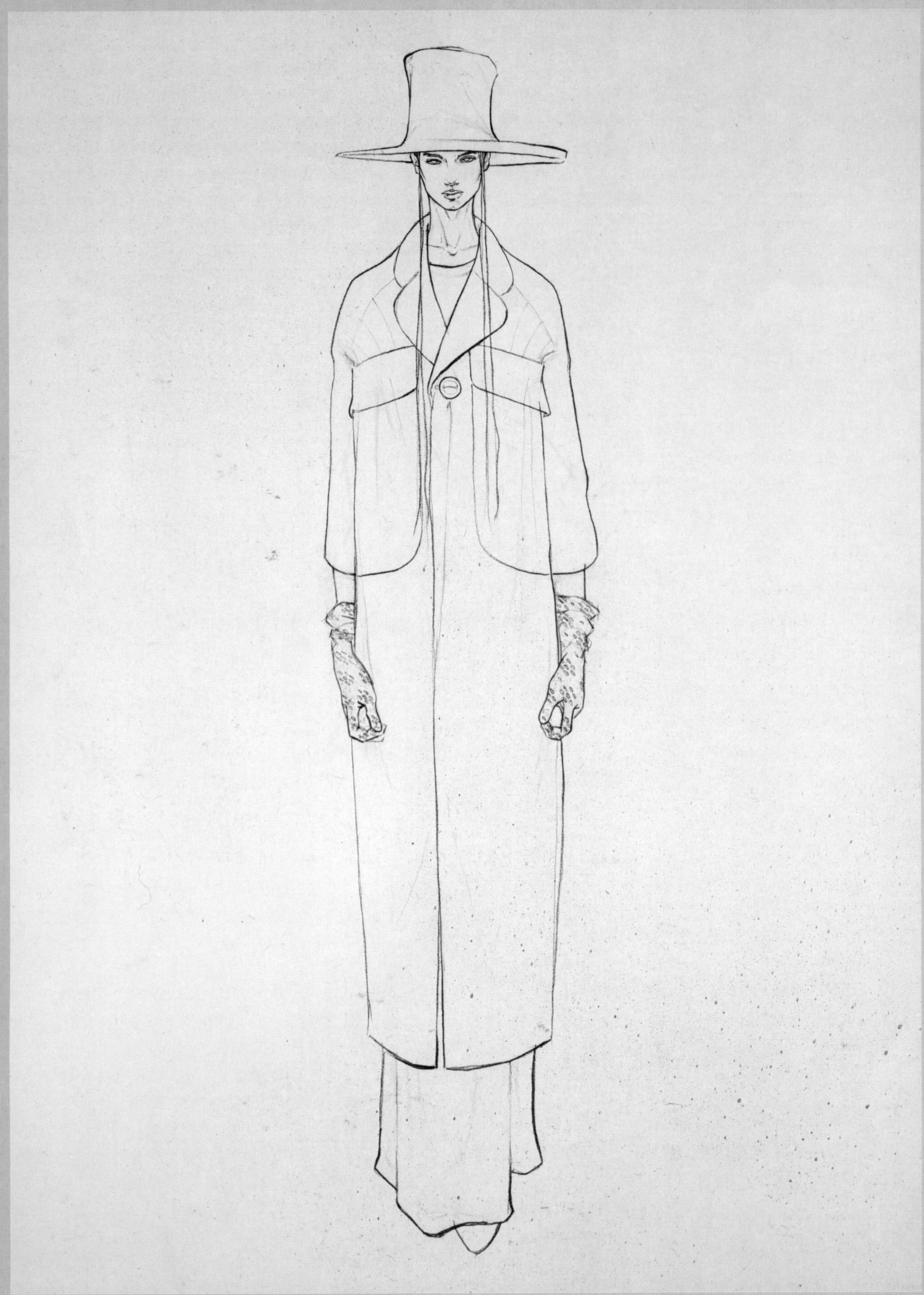

It is forgotten that John Galliano's clothes in the 1980s had a strong linear quality and a bold sense of scale. The result of a highly developed and precise fashion sense, they were the qualities which raised his work above that of all the other fashion wunderkind *jostling for attention in London at the time. (Drawing Claire Smalley)*

of the clothes. It is the culmination of at least a month's involvement from John and his team, looking at Polaroids, making colour tests, checking fabric swatches and approving artefacts that will dress the set. As with the dresses, the music, and every other aspect of the show, nothing about the venue is left to chance. It is rightly seen as the vital setting for that once-only opportunity to sell the Galliano story, in all its ramifications, for the coming season.

There are others outside the house whose role in the selling process is crucial: the make-up and hair specialists; the shoemaker and the milliner. Stephen Jones has created hats for Galliano shows since John moved to Paris, including his Givenchy and Dior collections. Although the hats are produced especially for the show and do not go into production, they are seen as a vital part of the Galliano projection. As Stephen Jones says, 'A hat can kill an outfit completely – or it can make it. John takes hats very seriously. He sees them as integral to his clothing statement. He dresses the woman in his head and the hat requires as much effort as any other part of the collection.'

He has his first discussions about five weeks before the show. 'John talks me through the collection. It's a wonderful performance. He explains very carefully what the collection is about – the themes, the places, the time, and masses of widely different references. The initial briefing can stretch to four or five hours of talk. At that point, John has the outfits numbered on blank pieces of white paper, but nothing drawn. There will be sourcebooks everywhere and maybe one or two preliminary sketches of a jacket shape or a silhouette. I take notes, but they're not important. What matters is catching the spirit, although I don't always come away with a strong idea of where the collection is likely to go.'

of discipline. He has exquisite refinement and a wonderfully fine eye, but what is marvellous about him is his ability to trigger ideas and begin thought processes. It's amazing how focused and efficient he has become since moving to Dior. Very to the point.'

Blahnik's role does not require the same close involvement as Stephen Jones's does. In fact, he and John understand each other sufficiently for the shoe story to evolve from only one meeting and a few telephone calls. Like Stephen, Manolo makes his *toiles* and then he sends them to John. He recalls the pleasure he had in making the shoes for John's debut couture collection for Dior, shown in January 1997: 'I had such a wonderful time working on it – it was like being on holiday. I was in Venice and John sent me pictures of the Masai. I was especially excited by the head-dresses, so I decided to adapt them to sandals that would coil up the leg. I rushed around Venice buying all the different tiny beads I could find. Then I made a *toile* and stuck them on it by hand, using UHU glue. Everybody was saying, "You can't do this! It's crazy." But John was very excited and said, "As it's African, what about some fur?"' I said, "Give me some! Some chinchilla!" In the end they looked like naughty little animals, ready to bite!'

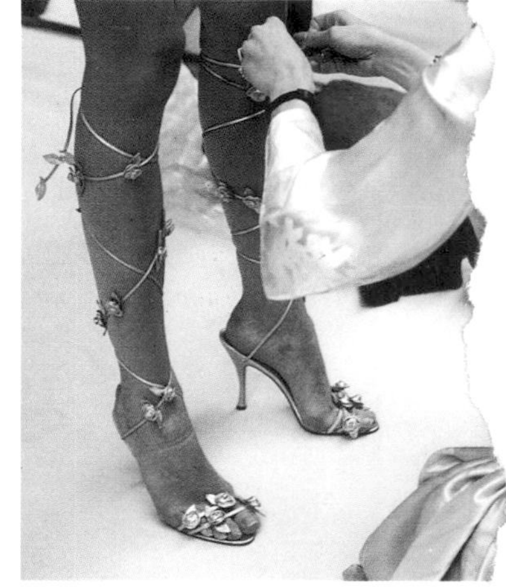

It is the fantasy of John Galliano that appeals to Manolo but, as a highly commercial designer, he responds to the fact that, 'underneath all the amazingly

'For the Dior show, the hair was so complicated that Odile had to have her team do the hair for all the magazine fashion shoots. She kept her entire team – which comes from all over the world – in Paris for an extra week and sent them out with each of the magazines. Odile has a large team but they inspire and understand each other. Above all, they understand her and her demands, which is important, as she can't possibly do every girl's hair herself. In many cases all she has to do is check and tweak a bit. Her team is marvellous. They've been coming for years and they still go out and find a McDonald's because they hate French food! We love that!'

Another person who fields a big team and starts working with John in advance of the show is Stéphane Marais, who conceives the make-up. They have worked together for eight years and have total mutual trust. The process starts well in advance with a brief conversation between the two men. From this, Stéphane will begin to have ideas of how the make-up should be, but he prefers to keep his proposals in his head until he has seen the clothes. 'I know what his feelings and inspirations are,' he claims, 'so I know the sort of feeling he wants the make-up to have. The night before, with the final fittings, I stay very late and I like to surprise him – you know, maybe I can see something at the last moment. And John always says, "Do it."'

The day of the show, when all the work, theorizing, research and discussions come to fruition, is a long one. It starts at around seven in the morning, with Steven Robinson and Vanessa arriving at the venue, which they may only have left a few hours before, having worked virtually the entire night through. The next two hours are spent checking every detail of the clothes, making sure that all the accessories are with them and everything is ready to be put on. For a show scheduled at eight in the evening, the first girls will arrive at eight in the morning. The teams of hair and make-up artists begin to work with them. The newer girls arrive early; others are in by about eleven and the supermodels will arrive by two – the very latest time for an evening show. As John Galliano says, 'There's a whole hierarchy thing going on with the girls and the make-up and hair people with which I never get involved. There are too many forces going on. The girls know their moment – when to make eyes at a certain make-up artist. It's all very eighteenth-century, like Versailles. The younger girls are looking and learning. The ones who've been there for ages won't go to Stéphane's seat. They *daren't* take that chair. Naomi will.'

It is a day which flies by. The girls talk, snooze, have their boyfriends and family in, and endlessly telephone. They sit for over an hour while false hair is sewn in – there are no wigs used. They all want Odile's hand and the master make-up touch of Stéphane. In fact, each specialist brings a team of a dozen or more hair and make-up artists. There are considerable numbers behind the scenes by mid-afternoon, fifty girls, each with a dresser, all the make-up and hair artists, security men, pressers, coffee-makers, technicians, family, friends, hangers-on, TV cameras and their crews; the atmosphere becomes sharper, more anticipatory; the mood swings from ordered chaos to controlled partying. Everyone is aware that the feeling must be kept lively if the show is to have the spirit and life to take the audience with it. Theatricality starts long before the show commences.

'We tell the story at the fittings,' John says. 'The whole story, not just the individual girl's part. The walk. The attitudes. They study the dress. They like

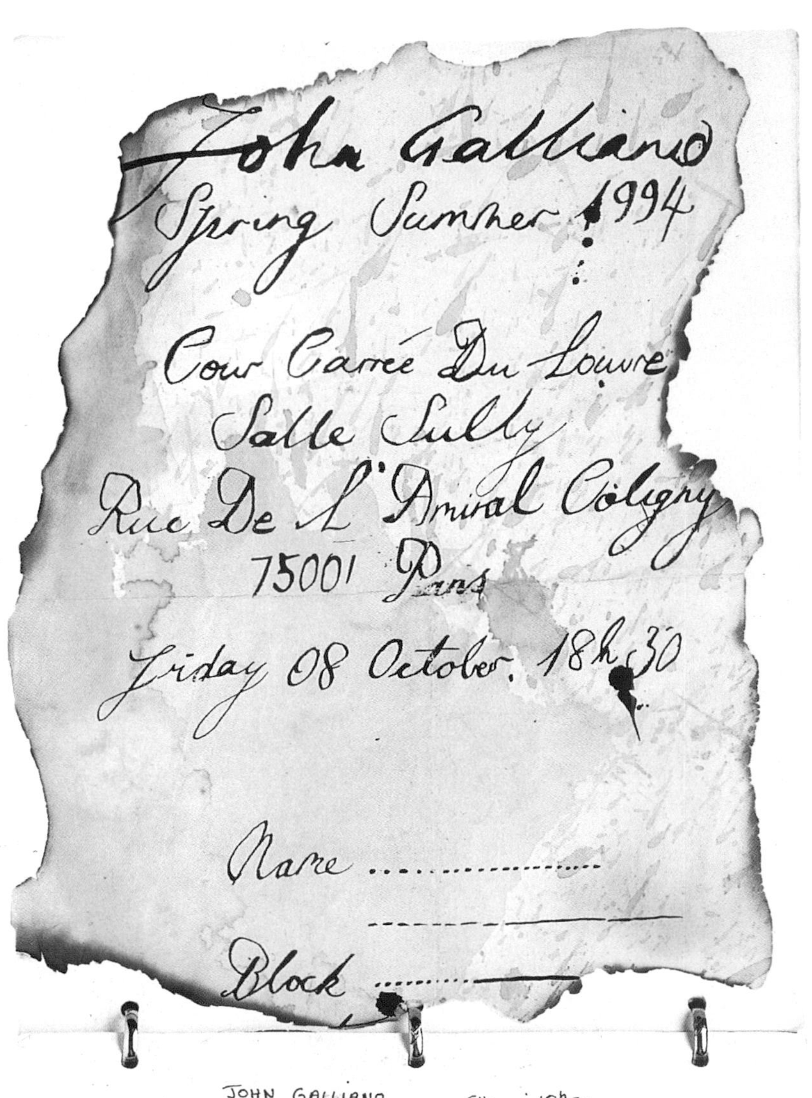
John Galliano
Spring Summer 1994

Cour Carrée Du Louvre
Salle Sully
Rue De L'Amiral Cóligny
75001 Paris

Friday 08 October. 18h30

Name ....

Block ....

JOHN GALLIANO Show à 18h30

RDU à: 13h30 Cour Carrée. Salle Sully.

direction but their personalities are really important so I encourage them to interpret it all in a way that is right for them. They find their way. What they can't be is timid. They don't get a second chance. I tell them, "It's your one outfit, honey. You only get one shot! Go for it!" And they know it. They worry terribly.'

During the day, John takes each girl through the rooms for an individual rehearsal. 'Here's a good place to pause.' 'Why don't you lie on that couch for a minute before you go on? The photographers can see you there.' 'Lean against this tree.' It's theatre and John rehearses it to fit each girl's personality. 'They get nervous,' Steven says. 'They are so frightened of letting John down. His method makes many more demands

Stéphane Marais is one of the world's leading make-up artists, responsible for the appearance of many of the top Parisian couturiers models. He works with the same painstaking care as Galliano does to ensure that his team is aware of all the historic references behind the make-up he creates to enhance the spirit of each show. (Right, photo: Christian Dior archive)

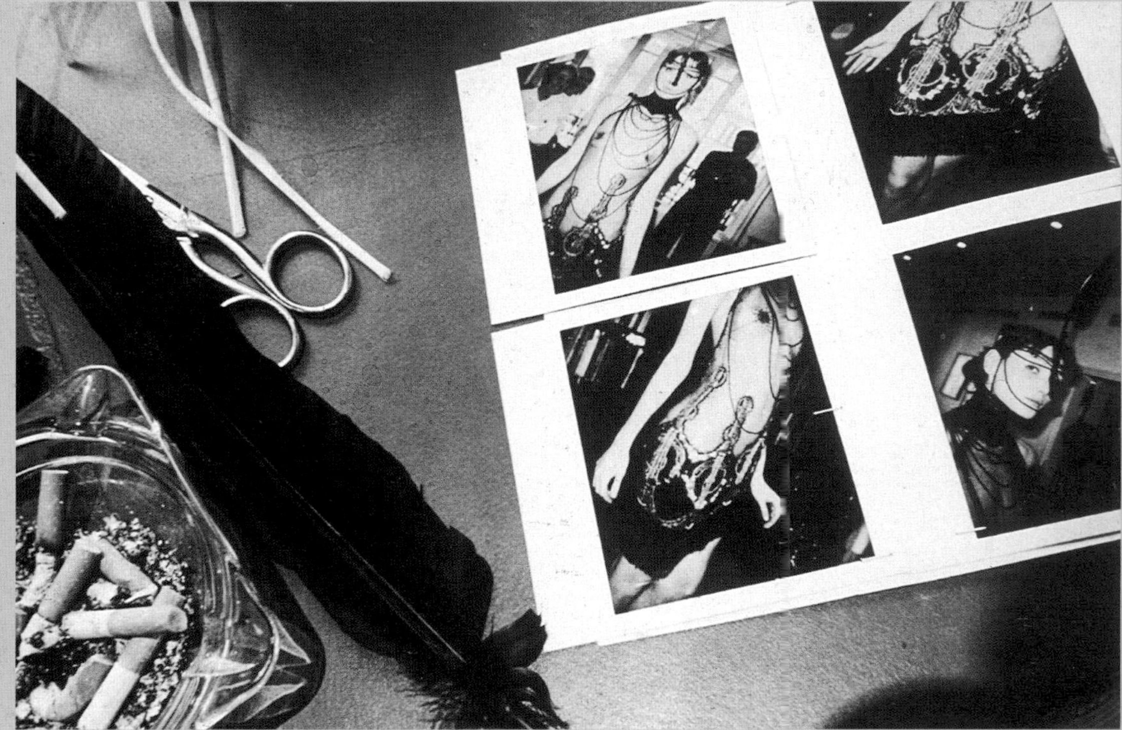

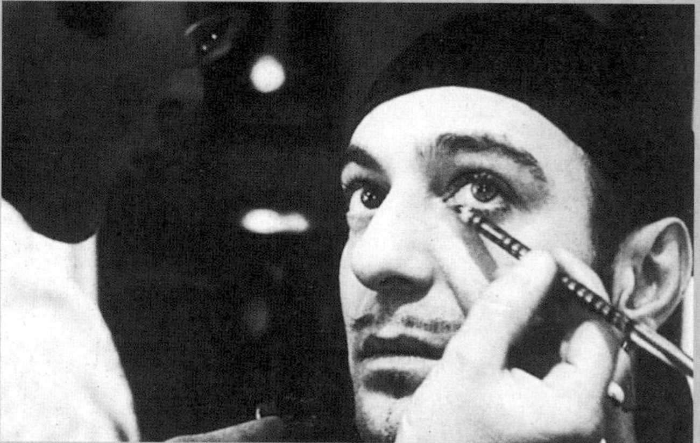

CARLA 30
SHIRLEY 31
ASTRID 32

12
Naomi

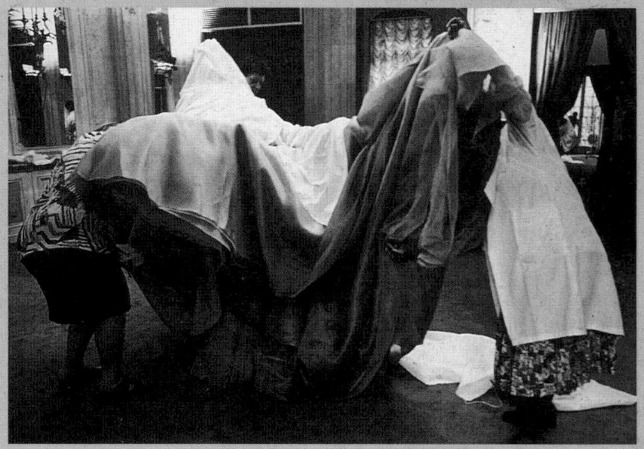

called in to help cope with demand. The press officer was sorting out pricing; John was doing the selling; his assistant was organizing confirmations with the shops and, in between, they were all frantically laying the patterns out on any space available throughout the mansion, grading them for size to enable the factory to get some sort of production going to begin satisfying the demands.

For a few days, the Schlumberger *hôtel particulier* was the Galliano headquarters, until a suitable space was found in the Passage du Cheval Blanc. The Galliano headquarters were up two flights of twisting stairs, in a very cramped space, but at least they were a proper space that could be permanently organized. The showroom was at the end of the cul-de-sac, and it was to be here that women made their pilgrimage: Nan Kempner, Anne Bass, and all the rich and

CREATIVELY, PARIS IS THE most accommodating of all Europe's cities, welcoming artists from around the globe and affording them the tolerance and freedom to find their own fulfillment. It is especially open to fashion designers. Charles Frederick Worth, considered the father of modern couture, was an Englishman who arrived in the city in 1845 and eventually became the world's most famous couturier.

In this century, it was to Paris that the Italian, Schiaparelli; the American, Mainbocher; and the Irishman, Molyneux; came to make their names. Most famously, it was to Paris that Balenciaga, arguably the greatest couturier since Worth, turned after London had rejected him in the late thirties when he was looking for sanctuary from the Spanish Civil War. And it was to Paris that John Galliano looked for a future that seemed increasingly unlikely to be safeguarded in London.

A timeless study of the beauty of John Galliano's vision of femininity, in his spring/summer 1994 collection. (Photo: David Seidner)

Galliano's move to Paris released a nw creative force in him, as his work became increasingly complex in cut and scale: fabrics acted and reacted against each other to produce a unity which, despite its apparent simplicity, was a marvellously controlled exercise in dressmaking at its highest point. (Drawings by Julie Verhoeven from Galliano's autumn/winter 1994–5 collection)

The many faces of Galliano glamour show how wide a creative spectrum he works within. Although there are many different moods in these clothes, they all share one thing: complete artistic authority.

Clockwise from top left: Galliano, spring/summer 1994 (Niall McInerney); Galliano, spring/summer 1993 (Patrice Stable Agency); Galliano, spring/summer 1996 (both Niall McInerney). This page, below: Galliano, spring/summer 1995 (Niall McInerney); opposite: Gallliano spring/summer 1995. (Niall McInery)

417
HF M7

Evening glamour takes many forms, from the exotically bouffant to the slinkily clinging, but whether it is a question of controlling many yards of material, or cutting on the bias a dress which highlights every nuance of the figure, Galliano has mastered both skills. (Photos: Patrick Demarchelier)

John Galliano's forte is the bias-cut satin dress. No one has done it better since Mme Vionnet first invented the technique in the 1920s. This deceptively simple but consummate example of the art is worn by Linda Evangelista, and is from the Galliano spring/summer 1994 collection. (Photo: Steven Meisel)

The thing which makes Paris unique in the world's fashion capitals is not only the range and nationality of its designers but also its infrastructure of craftsmanship, without which work to the highest level of couture is impossible. It is in Paris that the fingers of the cleverest workers in feathers and beading are found. The manufacturers of buttons and trims reach a standard there that can be found nowhere else. It is this city alone that produces the most exquisite ribbons in colours bolder or more subtle than those found elsewhere. Paris is the city which can turn the most far-fetched designer fantasy into reality. It was this city which was to revitalize John Galliano with its attitudes and give him hope for his future.

John was no stranger to Paris. He had held his first show there in 1989 and had already been selling there in order to reach a wider audience. 'I was ready for it,' he recalls. 'It was an adventure. I had contacts here and, of course, Steven came with me.' Steven Robinson adds, 'We already had a press officer in Paris. So, we thought, what should John do to get over to Paris? We were prepared to go backwards and forwards until we found backers but the move happened virtually overnight. London was dead. Nothing was happening. John said, "We're moving." And we did. Faycal believed in John and he made it all possible.' 'I knew I'd stay,' John continues. 'I was committed to Paris. I knew that I could make my dreams come true there.'

Faycal Amor faced John's problems head on, with instant practicality. As the designer-owner of the Plein Sud sportswear label, he was able to provide backing: a public relations organization and a computerized clothing factory, where it was planned to manufacture Galliano's Girl, the casual, jeans-based range that had first been mooted when John was at Aguecheek. Amanda Harlech saw a difference very quickly. 'John was able to develop new techniques because the Plein Sud factory had marvellously sophisticated machinery and a highly technical staff. They had faggoting machines which produced amazingly delicate work. It was marvellous for John. He was able to use really good fabrics for the first time in his career. Things like leather and brocade. But it came with a price-tag. Suddenly design integrity was less of a teeth-grinding issue than production, it seemed to me.'

John points out, 'I learned a lot from Faycal. He was so practical. He showed me how to secure my labels – although there were complications with that, as he gave his address on the documents – and he taught me about mass manufacture. At the end of the day, Galliano's Girl didn't catch on. The price difference between it and the main range was too small, people went for the real thing. It turned Galliano into a house with two heads.'

Galliano's first Paris show in 1989, immediately after Aguecheek had pulled out, had been a shoestring affair. 'We had literally to make the collection out of paper,' Amanda Harlech told US *Vogue*. But, under Amor's umbrella, things loosened up a lot. John's studio consisted of eight people who did everything, including taking time to do the washing-up and Hoovering.

Despite the artistic success of his collections, difficulties with his backer meant that, by 1993, John was alone again with only his team to support him. He slept on friends' floors and he borrowed money for the Métro. But that didn't worry him in the least. He looks back and says philosophically, 'My life has all been twists and turns but it's had its moments – magic moments.' What really hurt him after parting company with Amor was that he was unable to stage a show. Even now, in his success, it pains him: 'I missed a season, and that was terrible.'

But the magic moments were to return. 'We'd made quite an impact with the Olivia Philibustier show for Spring–Summer 1993, especially in America. Anna Wintour, editor-in-chief of American *Vogue*, and André Leon Talley, *Vanity Fair*'s European correspondent, became great fans. I'd reached the point where I wanted my independence, to have my own house. People knew that I was deadly serious and that I wouldn't go on working as I was. I was seeing various people about backing, including Italians.' It was after a trip to Milan that he had dinner with Anna Wintour, who was appalled by the situation he was in.

Editors of great fashion magazines are not always renowned for gentleness or sentimentality. They are generally considered one of the tougher sub-species of *Homo sapiens*. But what they all share is not just a shrewd fashion judgement, a response to beauty and a respect for talent, but also an ability to judge a situation practically, and to take action. Anna Wintour was no exception.

Her advice was crisp and incontrovertible. 'You cannot miss another season. You must do something,' she urged. To John it seemed madness. There were four weeks before the collections. He had no studio and no money. But he knew she was right. What he perhaps didn't know is that the path to editor-in-chief of a major magazine is no primrose-strewn country lane. It is the hardest, most dangerous *autostrada* in the world. It makes the person who successfully negotiates it not only determined but resourceful. The Wintour rescue operation began that night.

Firstly, she did what powerful women usually do to start the ball rolling: she arranged a lunch. André Leon Talley took John to meet São Schlumberger, a Portuguese socialite, for what was to be the first of what became known as the 'staff lunches' with her at which, John recalls, she served fantastic Portuguese sardines. André asked her if she might be prepared to lend her eighteenth-century *hôtel particulier* as a venue for a show. She had already bought from Galliano and was a devoted follower of couture, having consistently patronized Givenchy, Dior and Chanel in the past. Even so, her answer surprised John. 'Yes, why not?' she responded straight away.

It was the turning point. From that show on, held in the empty mansion which had been up for sale for some time, no Galliano collection would ever be shown in humdrum or predictable surroundings again. But before the show could take place, a backer needed to be found. Anna Wintour arranged for John to be flown

The quintessential Romantic ballgown by Galliano for Givenchy. Monumental yet fluid, it is high fashion at its traditional best. (Photo: Lillian Bassman)

OK
NADJA
BAZAAR

Previous page: The way in which a dress is shown on the catwalk is evolved in rehearsals by the interaction of the personalities of the designer, the model and the dress. Givenchy haute couture, spring/summer 1996, designed by John Galliano. (Photos: Andrew McPherson)

The ethereal recreation of the quality of an Ingres painting may, at first glance, make this dress appear almost like a costume, until the eye notices the complex beauty of the tiny jacket, which is totally modern and uniquely Galliano. (Galliano, spring/summer 1994; photo: David Seidner)

then up in the special lift to the top floor. There I was ushered into a huge room. There was one big table and all that was on it was a bottle of mineral water and two glasses. Suddenly there was this amazingly elegant figure in grey. He had very strong, young eyes and controlled, small movements. I showed him my research books and explained how I worked. My hair was long – I had dreadlocks then – and I had to keep trying to press it down. I was impressed with how well he had been briefed. He knew everything already.'

What Arnault was most interested in knowing was how Galliano would sustain interest after the first two collections, when the novelty had gone. 'I talked about finding the identifiable moments in Givenchy's career. Once the meeting had started, I relaxed. I knew this was just a formality. I'd already been checked out and I'd met all of the Givenchy hierarchy. People had been giving Galliano the once-over for weeks, checking deliveries, the quality of the work and everything to make sure we weren't a flaky prospect. They were *very* thorough.' The appointment was announced in July 1995.

Galliano has since wondered if Givenchy was already seen by Arnault as a rehearsal for Dior. If it was, no hint was given at the meeting which finalized the deal, and John started immediately by looking closely at Givenchy's career, searching for 'moments', although he couldn't use the archives until Givenchy had actually left. Although he fully understands the sensibility of Christian Dior, he found it much more difficult to identify answering chords in Givenchy. 'But I was basically so happy just to have the set-up to work within, to be able to do couture, that I knew it would be all right. I had to learn to work within the Givenchy structure. I'd never been in a couture establishment before, let alone been in charge of one. But the people in the ateliers were marvellous.' Hubert de Givenchy had been an old-style couturier, very formal and dignified. He wore the traditional white overall when

Evening glamour can be on a lavishly eighteenth-century scale or as delicate as a filigree shawl from the belle époque. In either case, it is their total femininity which gives these dresses their appeal. Left and right: Givenchy haute couture, spring/summer 1996, designed by John Galliano. (Photos: B. Pellerin, Givenchy archive)

Galliano, autumn/winter 1995–6. (Photos: Patrice Stable Agency)

working, but always beneath it was a city suit and an immaculately knotted tie. He kept a distance between himself and the atelier staff. Galliano broke that tradition on the first day by eating in the staff canteen. 'Lentils and fish – and sixty pairs of eyes on me!' he recalls. And, of course, his dress codes were notoriously free and easy.

The pressing need was to make the Givenchy line look younger. It seemed to Galliano that Givenchy's approach was too couture-dictated, even in his ready-to-wear. 'He was temperamentally always designing with his private customers in mind. He just didn't have a prêt-à-porter angle. The clothes had to be given a broader appeal for the shops.' But before that could be tackled, there was a couture collection to be designed, to be shown in January 1996, and the Galliano collection to be prepared for the October 1995 Paris shows.

The Galliano show was held at the Théâtre des Champs Elysées, famous as the venue for the Ballets Russes in 1913, and the scandal of *Le Sacre du Printemps*, which was premiered there. Galliano's staging exploited the theatrical possibilities of the space by placing members of the audience on stage, including Paloma Picasso, Inès de la Fressange, Azzadine Alaïa and Gianfranco Ferré, and having the models move

Galliano, spring/summer 1993. (Photos: Patrice Stable Agency)

among the guests in the auditorium. The overall theme was a ballet school at rehearsal time. As *The New York Times* described it, 'There was a ballet bar with prepubescent ballerinas doing *pliés* in front of a mirror, a make-up table cluttered with wadded Kleenexes, a woman with a *pince-nez* playing the piano, stacked wicker baskets exploding with tulle,' and, drifting through it all were clothes which *Women's Wear Daily* called, 'the most exquisite anyone has seen in Paris this season... He can do the most elaborate taffeta ballgowns or the simplest black pelmet jacket... and make them look like no other designer's – before or now.' As the *New York Times* said, 'It had the sort of edge that propelled Mr Galliano to authority...' – an authority which had brought him the award of British Designer of the Year for a third, unprecedented, time and Spain's most prestigious fashion accolade, *Telva* magazine's Designer of the Year Award, both in 1995.

It was this authority which Bernard Arnault was expecting in January 1996. He nearly didn't get a Givenchy couture show at all, as Paris was paralysed by an eighteen-day strike shortly before the shows. 'It was a nightmare,' Galliano recalls. 'The women in the ateliers had to walk to work. Paris was one huge traffic

jam… You couldn't move. The atmosphere was scary. Thinking of strikes in London, Steven and I kept saying, "Will it *ever* stop?" But it was so Paris: the men in the *tabac* and the taxi-drivers only cared about football and the couture. Nothing else mattered.'

Despite Karl Lagerfeld's prediction that couture week would have to be cancelled, the shows went on and, on 21 January 1996, the Galliano for Givenchy show took place in the Stade Français with 50 girls and five stage sets before an audience that included socialites such as Jacqueline Delubac and Bettina Graziani and stars like Tina Turner and Joan Collins. It contained a cleverly judged mixture of the fantastic – long-trained evening dresses on the theme of the Princess and the Pea – and the desirable – beautifully cut suits in silk crepe. It prompted a laudatory editorial in US *Vogue*'s March collections issue: 'These were the most exciting collections in a long time,' wrote Anna Wintour. 'This was the first time that I can remember there was a measure of suspense to the couture. Could the London *wunderkind* with the cockney accent and the ever-changing hair-dos pull it off?… We should congratulate Bernard Arnault… for having the guts to do something as daring as this.' It was the final seal of approval on all the earlier favourable comments on the show – unanimous except for the *International Herald Tribune*, which had condemned John's Givenchy debut as 'a fashion moment that missed'.

For his own Galliano label show, John chose the Polo de Paris riding stable in the Bois de Boulogne in which to recreate an Indian settlement. 'Honcho Woman' opened with a horse galloping wildly down the sanded catwalk, which was marked with Indian signs and the abandoned detritus of an imposed culture – the fender of a Wyoming-registered Cadillac, cast-off oil barrels and abandoned tyres. The show, which Galliano described as 'a mix of the Duchess of Windsor and the Hopi Indians', was praised by *Women's Wear Daily* as

Left: Galliano, spring/ summer 1993; above: Galliano spring/ summer 1997. (Photos: Niall McInerney)

The Orient has a powerful pull on Galliano. Pagoda hats, Far Eastern fabrics and uncompromising make-up recall Chinese opium dens in the 1920s. Galliano, spring/summer 1997. (Photos: Paolo Roversi)

High-gloss glamour revisited. John Galliano's reworking of the world of 1950s chic conjures visions of the elegant creations of Dior, Fath and Balmain, as worn by the models of the time, Suzy Parker and Lisa Fonssagrives. Galliano spring/summer 1995. (Photos: Mario Testino)

'He creates a total world – the magic world of John Galliano – unlike the spirit of any other fashion designer.'

– ODILE GILBERT

Galliano, spring / summer 1997, worn by Naomi Campbell. (Photo: Paolo Roversi)

'Galliano at his Galliano best… rich, imaginative and romantic.' Galliano himself brought it down to earth by telling journalists that his heroine was a 'proper little squaw on her podium, straightening her seams'.

By the time Galliano was ready to present his next collection, in October 1996, it was known that his period at Givenchy was to be cut short. In fact, he created two prêt-à-porter and one couture collections for the house before gathering the glittering prize and moving to Dior. If there was a slightly valedictory feeling to his last show for Givenchy, his own line was stronger than ever. His circus spectacular, staged in an empty wine warehouse, was one of the most semantically complex shows he had ever produced. Jeremy Healy, who has created the music for Galliano shows since the first St Martin's eight minutes in 1984, and John's oldest collaborator and friend, remembers his brief as a 'story about a Russian gypsy called O'Flannagan', as the show became known. The show had Romanian gypsy bands, tightrope walkers, trapeze artists and accordion players creating an atmosphere redolent of the film-maker Fellini, or the thirties photographers Josef Koudelka and Henri Cartier-Bresson. The clothes were as spectacular as the circus setting created by Jean-Luc Ardouin: biker's jackets, diaphanous bias-cut gowns heavy with embroidery, ethnic patterns and Wedgewood chinoiserie showed how Galliano's hand was strengthening.

His success was summed up by Anna Wintour in a South Bank television programme devoted to his Paris years, culminating in his first show for Givenchy when she pointed out, 'There are few truly creative people in the fashion world who, through their spirit, their creative joy and their personalities, really give fashion what it needs – some inventive madness.'

CODA: The Faces of John Galliano

JOHN GALLIANO HAS BEEN a fashion designer for a dozen years, since his first commercial fashion show, the Ludic Game, in March 1985. Although he has already worked under his own name for two years longer than Christian Dior did, he has, in all probability, covered no more than a quarter of his life as a top fashion designer. And, of course, he has lived it in the full glare of publicity which lit on him in the summer of 1984, with his graduate show, and has never been switched off since. Public interest in the man and his fashion philosophy was captured at the outset, and time has done nothing to change it.

Such fame so soon brings its rewards, but it has its disadvantages. Christian Dior achieved his own fashion house only at the age of forty-two, by which time he had made his mistakes and learned his strengths and weaknesses anonymously, working as an assistance to other designers. His New Look was no tyro effort, even if it was his first solo collection. It was the work of a matured design mind, a brilliant eye, and a steady hand perfected over many years. It laid a foundation on which Dior could possibly have built for at least another twenty years, had he not died of heart failure in 1957, ten years after his debut.

SNOWDON

It would have been twenty years of remarkably consistent clothes, emanating from a tried-and-tested fashion approach, a fixed belief in what was good and bad in fashion and in taste, and a strongly felt credo about how a woman of style should dress. There would have been seasons that were surprising, but none that presented a shock, seasons that disappointed, but none that failed.

One of the marks of a genius in any field is the ability to remain consistent without becoming dull, and to delight with the unexpected without alarming with the unfamiliar. That is what gives the creator his handwriting. We expect always to be able to recognize a Michelangelo. We don't want a Monet to look like a Cézanne. We would be confused if a Brontë novel read like one by Jane Austen. We would feel short-changed if, after a couple of lines, we didn't know whether the poetry we were reading was by Dylan Thomas or Robert Frost. We don't want inconsistency in our creators. Reliability is the key to opening the door of the pantheon of greatness.

The tendency to instant fame which has characterized all fields of endeavour, from sport and music to art and fashion, in the past thirty years, makes life difficult for people like John Galliano. Although they get opportunities and rewards far earlier than their predecessors, they have to do their creative growing-up in public. Who is the real John Galliano, dress designer and couturier – the man of the eighties, or the man of the nineties?

The eighties Galliano was in love with 'windblown romance' – the world of Heathcliff and Cathy, all doomed passion under lowering northern skies, their clothes torn and dishevelled by riding hard through groves of thorns and over drystone walls; their hair deranged by howling winds. The Ludic Game, Fallen Angels and Forgotten Innocents are to many the quintessence of Galliano's vision: fresh, young, and remarkably pure. Characterized by bravura, a finely balanced sense of scale and the courage to modernize old techniques and historic approaches, they were condemned by the unimaginative as fancy dress, costume, even pantomime, but adored by the rest as original, adventurous and, above all, entirely modern.

Forgotten Innocents was shown in 1986, but its marvellously confident cutting, and the liquefaction of its line marked the end of a way of thinking. Big shapes would soon become big details, such as the large bows and cascading skirts of his 'Blanche Dubois' collection for Spring–Summer 1988, as the body became more emphasized and the shapes became tighter and more contour-close.

But historicism continued. The fascination with uniform which had first manifested itself in his Incroyables degree show continued with 'Napoleon and Josephine' in 1992. Large collars with broad, flat lapels in 'sans-culotte' stripes; high, cascading hair, feathers and lace created a collection more overtly 'sexy' than anything previously done by Galliano. Like his degree show, it had a feeling of violence having been done. It seemed that his women, with their frayed and fretted hemlines and torn and fragmented laces hanging awry, were the survivors of some maelstrom, and while, as survivors, they paced their space like panthers or even Amazons, they exhibited none of the *joie-de-vivre* of the earlier survivors which was so uplifting in his degree show. The clothes were beautiful but the thinking confused – and the reaction in the audience exhibited as much unease as joy.

Not for the first time, the question was asked: what

attitude to modern women lies behind these ravishing but deeply unsettling clothes? It was a question the couturier went some way towards answering with his Spring–Summer 1993 collection, Olivia the Philibustier. He came down firmly on the side of romance with dresses of an even more glamorous scale than in previous collections, a line of thought which came to complete fruition in his first Givenchy show, with evening dresses spreading out into magnificent trains several metres long.

It was an affirmation of a movement that had been apparent for some time: John Galliano's heroines lived in the hazy, middle European fastnesses: polonaise princesses; mazurka mistresses, their habitat was the secret cobbled courtyard, the hidden door in the flaking wall, the long disused stone staircase sweeping up to boudoirs whose shutters, thrown back, revealed panoramas of Prague... Warsaw... Vienna, while the breeze from the Moldau... Vistula... Danube rustled through the charred paper of the abandoned love-note and scattered the dead roses around the silver mirror which reflected the small but beautifully chased ivory-handled pistol lying on the leopard-skin covered chaise longue against the Coromandel screen.

For many of his collections in the late eighties and early nineties, it seemed touch and go as to whether Galliano's heroines would turn the pistol on themselves or use it to wreak vengeance on ravishers unknown. Were they the spurned ones, or were their lovers languishing in the wings, suffering the sweet agonies of rejection? It was a question not resolved by the 'Princess Lucrezia' collection for Summer 1994, seen by many as the final flowering of John's icon of the lady of refined appearance who was tremulous, aloof and only truly at ease in her own secret garden of the past. She was more. The sweet young girl in clinging chiffon who had epitomized the Galliano ideal of femininity in his first collections had grown up, exchanged innocence for allure, and was now confident in slinky satin and crepe de Chine.

Galliano had fallen in love with the richness of fabrics, the beauty of which he knew could only be fully exploited by clothes of the highest sophistication. The dryness of crepe, the liquidity of velvet and the sheen of satin demanded certain interpretations. Can innocence be clothed in bias-cut satin and survive? They were the precursors of a new allure, which would become increasingly sexy. Some Galliano followers were shocked at the highly idealized images of high-class Chinese brothels and Japanese houses of pleasure which had crept into his clothes. But, in fact, it was less the sexual than the exotic element of Orientalism which interested him.

He had discovered *Japonisme*, the late nineteenth-century artistic obsession with Japanese art which, beginning with the opening of Japanese ports to the world by Commander Perry of the U.S. Navy in 1858 (the man on whom Lieutenant Pinkerton was based in Puccini's *Madame Butterfly*), routed the reign of all things Chinese – which had powerfully gripped Holland and England since the early eighteenth century – and made artists everywhere attempt to copy the brilliance of newly discovered Japanese masters such as Hokusai. Walter Crane, Whistler, Manet and, supremely, Degas, were hugely influenced by *Japonisme* and, above all, the kimono, an integral part of the complex language of posture and gesture in the traditional Japanese Noh and Kabuki theatres.

Kimonos were worn in layers, the weight of their silks providing the swirling curves that give movement and animation to the garment. In his 'back from the brink' collection held at São Schlumberger's mansion in 1994, Galliano's use of the kimono was masterly. Taking the spirit behind the movement of the original garment, he gave it a totally nineties freedom, and defined his ideas of sexuality with brief diaphanous shifts cinched with wide obi sashes personifying the change which had been noted by his cutter Bill Gaytten. 'John's clothes have become hotter and raunchier under Steven's guidance,' he claims. 'John is romantic, Steven is obsessed with sexy youth – under his influence, skirts became very short, heels went right up and clothes became skin-tight.'

The linguistics of fashion always change in response to the latest stimuli; the tone of voice can vary considerably, even the vocabulary alters, but the basic language is formalized early in a designer's career. In Galliano's case, the emphasis may change with collections but the overall tone is consistent. By the early nineties, it was clear that the spirit of his collections would be taken from non-fashion stimuli: revolutions in spirit, politics and art; heroines from fiction, such as Blanche Dubois, and history, like the women photographed by Jacques-Henri Lartigue on lazy afternoons in Paris, the country, Deauville and Cannes; cultural clashes such as that between American consumerism and native Americans; artists ranging from Winterhalter to Georgia O'Keeffe.

It was equally clear that the richness of semantic references seen in the fabrication and accessorizing of his earliest collections had not been lost, even if they had been transformed. Homely linens and reliable tweeds were out, the richest and most precious of fine stuffs were in. Broken clocks and twigs in hair were replaced by exquisitely mannered headwear, almost too sculpturally perfect to be characterized by calling them anything as mundane as hats. There was a new sense of opulence and luxury. A voluptuous, even decadent, quality seemed to sever Galliano from his past but, in fact, it was the same voice speaking with an accent more refined and controlled and a vocabulary much more focused and precise.

The richness which delights many cloys the palate for some. They point out that the setting and props, the story-line that seems to take precedence over the clothes, and the theatricality of the John Galliano nineties shows threaten to overwhelm their purpose and make them appear an end in themselves, instead of a vehicle for selling clothes. They add that the need for spectacle is all on Galliano's side – the audience can do without it, but can he? Increasingly, the question is asked: is there a danger that the most innovative and experimental of all current fashion designers is being swamped by considerations not directly the concern of fashion? Is he turning into a fashion impresario, a ringmaster to his own private circus where, to fulfill a secret fantasy of womanhood, all he requires is gorgeous, scantily clad, women cantering and capering at his bidding?

The answer, for Galliano as much as those who raise such questions, might be found in those designers from the past who have most clearly, if subconsciously, influenced him – Paul Poiret, Elsa Schiaparelli, and Jacques Fath on one side; 'Coco' Chanel, Cristóbal Balenciaga and Charles James on the other. The first group is known for its creative exuberance; the second by its rigour.

Poiret was in love with the exotic, as is Galliano. He was a complex character with a convoluted personality, but he had a steadfast belief in his abilities and a rebellious streak which made him incapable of softening his revolutionary fashion approach. He was supremely arrogant and took little heed of money matters. He was the most influential of all couturiers in the first years of the century and reigned until the twenties, when he was toppled by Chanel. His achievement was to harness the erotic appeal of the exoticism of the Ballets Russes and Africa, and make them socially acceptable in fashion. He adored fancy dress.

Like Poiret, Schiaparelli had a genius for publicity, knowing exactly how to capture newspaper headlines with her eccentric, Surrealist-inspired fashions or her own larger-than-life behaviour, backed up by a stream of memorable *bons mots*. An eclectic borrower from the ethnic cultures of the world, she was able to take details from a wide range of sources and imbue them with her own sensibility. Paradoxically, she was in love with technology and capitalized on inventions new in her time, such as the zip fastener, to enable her to cut inventively. Diana Vreeland summed her up as bringing to the world of fashion 'daring, playfulness and fun', but, in fact, her skills were much more radical and far-seeing than she has been given credit for.

Almost forgotten is Fath, whose career was ended when it was at full strength by his death from leukaemia in 1954, aged forty-two. Known for his exaggerated scale and complexity of cut, he was also outstanding for his ability to control many different effects on one garment. His clothes were often judged eccentric because of their boldness but, in fact, they were always highly articulate examples of the arts of tailoring and dressmaking. Had he lived, he would have been a master on the level of Balenciaga.

It isn't possible to be a dress designer in the second half of the twentieth century and remain uninfluenced by the philosophy and success of Chanel. When Vreeland claimed that Chanel had invented the twentieth century for women she destroyed her point with hyperbole, but it is a truism that every garment worn by women today is, in some measure, a result of the thoughts, experiments and discardings of Chanel as she ruthlessly stripped away what she considered unnecessary decoration to uncover the root purpose of a garment suitable for modern women. Whereas she would condemn as the result of laziness the simple suits turned out in their thousands without thought or feeling by modern designers, who claim antecedents in her work, she would thoroughly approve Galliano's reworkings of classic shapes from the past in order to find his own truths, as she did. She would admire his rigour and respect his results, and might not necessarily find them too extravagant for her taste.

Certainly, she admired Balenciaga, the only contemporary whose name she felt worthy to be placed next to hers. She wasn't alone in her judgement. Balenciaga has been revered by every major couturier, from his great days in the forties and fifties up to the present. Reclusive, distant and forbidding in personality, he couldn't be further removed from the 'all-singing, all dancing' Galliano, but in creative spirit they are exceedingly close. They both bring to the creation of clothes a paradoxical approach. Their determination to tailor to perfection suggests the austerity of the obsessed, and yet their clothes are voluptuous, light as air and full of movement by turns. The two men share a superbly judged sense of drama, which results in clothes that make statements in their own right. Balenciaga once said that his customer required no taste, *he* would saddle her and send her out

'He is a perfectionist because he knows no other way. It has nothing to do with money. When he had no money, it was exactly the same. Getting everything perfect is much more important to him than eating or having a bed to sleep in. He could never cut corners for such trivial things.'

– STEPHEN JONES

into the world looking as perfect as a showhorse. Critics of Galliano sometimes say that the woman who wears his clothes is equally unimportant to him.

Charles James, seen by most fashion historians as, at the least, the technical equal of Balenciaga, viewed his customers as enemies who were always wanting to take away his creations before they were 'ready'. An obsessive perfectionist, he *never* felt they were ready. He was always convinced that the more time spent, the better the result – to use the term 'end product' would be inappropriate to a man who never contemplated an end. Eccentric, litigious, famously quarrelsome, Charles James was one of the greatest fashion experimenters of the century, working out the principles of cut and movement in fabric by an intricate series of calculations more akin to engineering than to the work of most fashion designers – calculations that would be entirely understood by John Galliano.

Galliano need be compared only with the greats of twentieth-century fashion, for that is what he has already proved that he will be. In fact, most fashion followers say that he has reached his level of excellence already. Certainly, there is a constancy in his work which suggests a creative maturity. Diverse, experimental, innovative and able to use history to his own ends, he combines the imaginative prodigality and the technical austerity of the very best of the past. The John Galliano of the nineties has grown, deepened and developed from the Galliano of the eighties. He seems set to enter the twenty-first century with the same energy, dedication and determination that, regardless of setbacks, he has shown in his career to date.

Glamour Preserved: ball gowns in protective dress bags, ready for their next appearance. (Photo: François-Marie Banier)

Fantastic HABERDASHERY

- 2725 (Fabric shop)